T5-AXJ-344

Not unto us, O Lord, not unto us, but unto thy name give glory, for thy mercy, and for thy truth's sake.

—Psalm 115:1

B
Ive

Home Before Dark

Margaret Johnson

Church Library
Shady Grove Baptist Church
Route One, Box 582
Carrollton, Georgia

914

ZONDERVAN PUBLISHING HOUSE OF THE ZONDERVAN CORPORATION
GRAND RAPIDS, MICHIGAN 49506

HOME BEFORE DARK
© 1978 by Margaret Johnson

Library of Congress Cataloging in Publication Data
Johnson, Margaret.
  Home before dark.
  1. Iverson, Janie Grimes.   2. Baptists—United States—Biography.   I. Title.
BX6495.I93J63   286'.1'0924 [B]   78-14957
ISBN 0-310-26680-7

All rights reserved. No part of this publication may be reproduced or transmitted in any form or by any means, electronic or mechanical, including photocopy, recording, or any information storage and retrieval system, without permission in writing from the publisher, except in brief quotations in reviews.

Printed in the United States of America

For Jeffrey

Acknowledgments

My deep appreciation for this book goes to Nancy Davis. She was the first to recognize that this story must be told and, after viewing a local TV talk show on which I was a guest, wrote me a letter unfolding her dream. I was immediately enthusiastic because, unknown to Nancy, I too knew and remembered Gerry and Janie Iverson when their first assignment was as Christian Education directors at our church. Through mutual friends I had followed their lives with joy, with sadness, and then to the hour of final shock.

I thank Nancy for her invaluable assistance—for researching facts, interviewing family and friends of the Iversons, transcribing tapes, and supplying me with information from her own rich friendship with Janie. She spent many days and nights at the typewriter until the manuscript was complete.

We are deeply indebted to Paul and June Grimes, who allowed painful and tender memories to surface as they relived deeply personal events of their lives so that Janie's story could be told.

We thank the Iversons' close friends Dick and Joanne Wagner and Don and Nancy Stitzel for their vividly remembered times and conversations.

A special recognition must go to Don and Carole MacLane for sharing scrapbooks, photographs, cards, and letters, which unfolded the story as though Gerry and Janie were writing it themselves. The MacLanes' friendship with the Iversons became an umbrella of love quickly sweeping over Jeffrey, offering him their very best—their love and their home.

We also wish to thank the MacLanes for the use of their cabin at Big Bear Lake, where Nancy and I could work uninterrupted long into the night and where we could retrace the Iversons' last day to the final tragic moment.

A thank-you to Vielka Kelly for her "Memories of Janie" and to Pam Nelson for her remembrances of a loving Janie, who comforted her after the birth of her own handicapped child. We also appreciate the help given by the Atwater Park Center for Disabled Children in remembering Nathan and his development.

We are most grateful to Dr. and Mrs. Roger Voskuyl, who graciously allowed us to write freely of their daughter Nancy's last day.

A deep appreciation goes to Eleanor Matthews, librarian of the First Baptist Church of La Crescenta, for her time and effort in locating tapes made by Gerry and Janie that were so vital to this book.

And lastly, we most gratefully say thank you to those who quietly prayed while we worked, which to us was the greatest gift of all.

The Iversons

Jeffrey, Krista
Gerry, Janie
Nathan

1

It was nearly dusk and the August sun, which had been broiling down relentlessly all day, was slipping behind the pine trees that outlined the mountains surrounding Big Bear Lake. It promised to be a perfect week in the southern California resort area. For Gerry and Janie Iverson the preparation for a long-awaited vacation had been hectic, but now that they were really on their way, the anticipation of retreating for five full days from a strenuous church calendar kindled a fresh happiness in the young pastor and his wife.

Janie shifted her hold on a bouncy two-year-old Nathan and let her hand slide into Gerry's. "Oh, honey," she breathed, "it's too good to be true. Just to be away with you and the children without any pressures or responsibilities. . . ."

"Or board meetings or late-night telephone calls," Gerry added, squeezing her hand. They smiled, and their eyes met in a tender glance.

"There'll be great fishing, kids." Gerry half turned and called to the children in the back seat. They leaned forward in excited expectation.

"Will we be there before dark, dad?" Jeffrey asked, and Gerry nodded, glancing at his watch. It was nearly six o'clock, but there should be plenty of time to reach the cabin at the top of the mountain, eat dinner, and settle in before night fell over the small village. They had passed numerous summer vacationers in campers and station wagons hauling boats along the hot stretch of freeway, but now they were at the turn-off leading to Big Bear City.

Lofty evergreen trees framed the sides of the winding road, wafting pungent scents of pine through the clear mountain air. The alpine trees seemed to kiss the blue sky. It was almost as though they were at the apex of the world. The little white Renault climbed the last hill, made a sharp turn onto a narrow road, and there at the end of the lane was the small rustic cabin nestled between towering pines, warm and welcoming.

Eleven-year-old Jeffrey climbed out first, excitedly lifting fishing gear from the back of the car, racing ahead to the cabin, trailed by his ten-year-old sister, Krista.

Gerry stood still for a moment, drinking in the twilight beauty of the lakeside, relishing the crisp coolness of the evening air. Everything about the mountains exhilarated him. The majesty and grandeur of the setting sun illuminated the sky behind the crowded pine trees on the sides of the mountains. They looked so small in the distance and seemed to be nodding to him that it was a week bright with promise. He sighed with happiness.

At first Gerry had put off all thoughts of a vacation this summer and especially this week when a crucial meeting had been scheduled, but Janie had gently persuaded him that he must get away for a time of rest. She was right. He was tired to the bone, weary from the "deep and hurting valley" of the past two years. Janie was holding Nathan, and a sudden tenderness brought Gerry to her side, his arm encircling her waist. They walked in silence together along the winding dirt pathway to the cabin, lost in their private thoughts. Even now the thought of Nathan's birth brought back the haunting anguish of the medical verdict, "Down's syndrome." It had been impossible to believe at that moment that their fair-haired "angel" would bring a new dimension of strength into their lives, deepening their love through the intense suffering they shared.

Janie set Nathan down and glanced around the room, a smile playing about her lovely mouth. At thirty-five Janie was a fragile beauty, softly feminine with short curly hair that framed her heart-shaped face. Sorrow had sweetened the expressive blue eyes, and it was part of her charm that a tenderness softened her beauty even more when she was alone with her family or spoke of them. But it was when she held Nathan that a kind of incandescence enhanced her face. Nothing could diminish it, not even wordless glances from passing strangers which seemed to say, "A mongoloid, what a shame." But they couldn't know the total joy Nathan had brought to their home.

At the beginning, when Gerry and Janie knew they had given birth to a handicapped child, cards and letters poured in with words of comfort. "God must have trusted you very much to leave Nathan in your care." After the first sharp pain of grief and disappointment, when they could "hear" once more, they knew it was true, and they felt that trust, holding it closely to them in a special private way.

During those first days after Nathan's birth, a mounting anguish of guilt had swept over Janie like raging tidal waves. She agonized over every minute of her pregnancy, wondering what she might have done to bear a child who was not perfect;

and when she could find no place where she might have failed and nowhere to lay the blame, another thought sprang into her mind—more frightening than any of the others. Had an inherited factor lay dormant in her body waiting to spring into seed in their unborn child?

When the first waves of nausea signaled her third pregnancy, Janie had verbally rejected the thought of another baby intruding into her beginnings of freedom now that Jeffrey and Krista were in school. She was excited about going back to work, dressing up each day, meeting new people, and bringing in a welcome addition to their income. All of that became a faded dream after Nathan's birth.

Even if she and Gerry had accepted Nathan's imperfections, what about Jeffrey and Krista? Were they ashamed and timid when strangers stared at them in public? Had Nathan's birth somehow scarred their other precious children?

Those were the very thoughts that had haunted Gerry in the beginning. As difficult as it was to admit even to himself, there was an unaccountable shame accompanying the birth of a handicapped child. When Jeffrey's and Krista's aptitudes had pushed them to the top 2 percent of their class, Gerry had felt a bursting pride. He had desired strong bodies and quick minds for his children, and now both were denied his second son. But that had been at first; lately his only concern was a deep longing to ensure Nathan's future.

And so a shadow had fallen over Gerry's life as he struggled out of the abyss of self-pity and despair. A thousand unutterable fears fiilled his thoughts, and only comforting passages from the Bible could dispel them: "As your days, so shall your strength be";[1] "Cast your burdens on the LORD, and he will sustain you."[2] Often his heart refused to grasp what his mind

---

[1]Deuteronomy 33:25b RSV.
[2]Psalm 55:22 RSV.

understood, but slowly his wounds were healing. He was learning to cast his burdens on the Lord and to live one day at a time, trusting God for wisdom to plan Nathan's tomorrows.

This week would be a special time alone with his family, all questions suspended. Don and Carole MacLane, close friends from high school and college, had invited them to use their rustic cabin. Food was placed in the refrigerator, clothing hung in closets, and boxes stacked along the wall. There would be time enough tomorrow to unpack and get settled.

Nathan ran in circles around the small living room, clapping his chubby hands until Janie caught him to her and held him close. "He's so wound up he'll never sleep tonight," she murmured to Gerry; and when he noticed her drawn face, he reached for Nathan.

"Let's go out and eat, honey," he said.

Jeff and Krista whooped in agreement and raced for the car. Janie smiled wanly, took one last look at the cozy warmth of the room, and turned to follow Gerry to the Renault. A week of blessed rest lay ahead, time to be with Gerry and the children— her dearest desire. She sighed contentedly and settled Nathan on her lap as Gerry started the car and headed down the mountain.

"We'll need film for the camera, Gerry," she reminded him softly, and he nodded.

"There's a grocery store at the edge of town. We'll stop there. I'd love to get a shot of this magnificent sunset." He looked toward the sky, then suddenly turned his head. "Hey, kids, what would you like to eat tonight?"

"Kentucky Fried!" they shouted in agreement, and Gerry laughed. He was beginning to unwind and turned to smile at Janie, reaching for her hand.

At the grocery store the children ran after Gerry, following him through the aisles pleading for candy or a special treat, but he was firm. Tonight they were only buying film.

"How about some gum, dad?" Jeff was already at the car, his hand on the door handle, still hoping to get a yes from his father. Gerry shook his head once more.

"Maybe tomorrow you can walk here and buy some gum, but not tonight. We're going to eat now and get a shot of the sky before dark. Into the car . . . we're on our way."

The white Renault backed up, turned, and carried the tired but happy family down the winding mountain road toward the village of Big Bear. It was 7:30 P.M. In a few minutes it would be dark.

In a pine-finished house in the heart of Big Bear, Bill Randolf had just finished his second beer and was about to switch on the television set for the evening news when the telephone rang sharply.

"Bill?" The voice on the other end was not a familiar one. "Bill Randolf?" There was alarm in the tone of the strange voice, and Bill sat up uneasily. "Hurry! Your place is on fire. We've already called the fire department, but you'd better hurry on down here."

Bill slammed the receiver into place and called out the news to his startled family, running ahead of his nephew Willie to the truck. Bill's heart was pounding as he started furiously down the winding mountain road. He was talking to himself. What had started the fire? Sure, it had been a dry season and fire was always a threat in the mountains, but Bill had never really believed it would happen to him.

He pushed his foot down harder on the accelerator, mumbling, "My lumber . . . my office . . . my papers . . . Oh, God . . . no . . . no . . .no!" He kept his foot to the floorboard; his thoughts racing wildly. In his mind he could envision his lumber being burned to the ground with all of his life's savings going up in flames.

Bill listened for the sound of fire trucks, but there were none.

He swerved sharply over the divider, turning the wheel abruptly to his side of the road. The next curve was a hazardous one, but he had driven this route daily for three years. Besides, at this time of night there should be little traffic.

His face was flushed with anxiety, his eyes probing the deepening dusk as he anticipated the next sharp curve.

Willie straightened suddenly and called out in terror, but Bill had already seen the danger. Just ahead a white Renault was slowly rounding the curve, and Bill had let his truck veer too far over the center divider. Instantly he saw that it was too late—they were going to collide head-on. In a flash Bill saw a stricken look on the driver's face; next to him a young woman was clutching a child.

The sound of metal upon metal crashed through the mountain air. Then there was a deadly silence.

Somewhere a fire was burning away Bill Randolph's life earnings, but now there was a greater fire in his brain. He was driven into frenzied action; he jumped from the truck, yelling at Willie to hurry . . . run to the call box, call the police, call the ambulance.

The white Renault lay on its side. In the back seat a little girl was moaning; a young boy, huddled in a corner, stared in a daze at Bill; the young couple and baby in the front seat were lifeless. Bill turned away in distress, clutching at the car and wishing desperately he could turn the clock back just a few minutes. Was it only ten minutes ago that he had been relaxing over a couple of beers, thinking how great life had become? Now he was engulfed in a nightmare, a twilight zone he could not escape. Tears were coursing down his cheeks as he talked gently to the boy, promising that help would be there shortly. "I'm sorry, I'm sorry," he kept saying over and over, but the boy didn't seem to hear him. His eyes were glazed and unseeing.

Willie was running back down the road, calling out that an

ambulance and a helicopter were coming. Willie halted sharply before the overturned car, his hands covering his mouth, his eyes widened in horror.

In the distance the sound of a fire truck was screaming toward Bill's lumberyard, but Bill didn't stir. He couldn't move from the boy's side, almost as though he could keep him alive by talking to him.

Time stood still for what seemed like forever before Bill could hear the distant whir of a helicopter. Down, down it came, circling like a giant bird. He watched transfixed while the paramedics lifted the girl from the car onto the stretcher and hurried back for the boy. Their faces were grave, and they simply shook their heads when Bill asked about the little girl.

As the screaming ambulance screeched to a halt by the overturned Renault, Bill sat on the ground and sobbed, his huge frame shaking convulsively. A patrol car pulled up beside him, and even though Bill knew he must compose himself and talk to the officers, he stayed on the ground weeping into his hands. He wanted to beg for forgiveness, but he didn't know who to ask.

It was dark now, and the scene was a bedlam of activity. Two newsmen had arrived, and one was setting up a TV camera. While the attendants lifted the bodies from the car, the camera was rolling.

"We'll get this on the eleven o'clock news," one of the men said dispassionately, and Bill got to his feet. He wanted to tear the camera from the man's hand and throw it savagely over the cliff, but he could only cling dizzily to the trunk of a tree.

The ambulance vanished, screaming through the darkness as it carried the bodies away. *What was life all about? If it could be snuffed out that fast, then what was it all about?*

In the distance billows of smoke and bursts of flames were shooting straight up into the sky. Bill had never insured his lumberyard properly, and now it was lost; yet how small that seemed compared to the sound of crashing metal and broken bodies stilled forever.

Who was this young family he had smashed to death? What dreams had they dreamed? *Why had it happened? Oh, God, why?* Their dreams had died with them and their hopes were buried forever. And he was responsible.

Bill was aware that a patrolman was waiting for him. He knew he would have to be driven to the station for questioning. But for one last dark moment he stood at the edge of the road, smashed his fist against the mangled Renault, and screamed across the mountain road into the blackness of the night:

"What is life all about? Somebody out there, tell me please, what is life all about?"

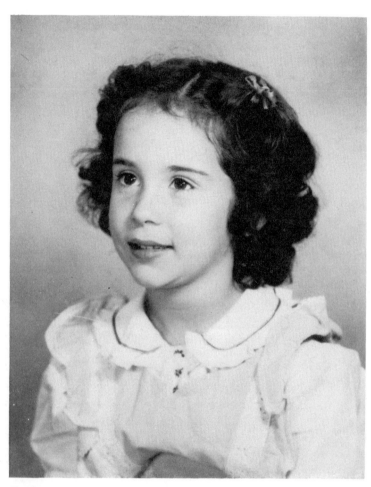

Janie

Helen Jane Grimes was born on a lovely morning in 1941 in the small California town of Montebello. It was April, and the spring rain of the past days had cleared the skies to a powder-blue, etching the distant mountains vividly against the heavens.

Her birth was a moment of fulfilled joy for Paul and June Grimes. In spite of repeated warnings by many doctors that June would never be able to bear a child, Paul and June had whispered their hearts' desire to their heavenly Father for five years, and now their hope and yearning had become reality. It was true—unbelievably, beautifully true.

The pregnancy had been a difficult one from the beginning, and in her third month the doctor warned June to banish all hope of carrying the baby to full term. But hope would not die. June lay in bed for the last six months, stabbing contractions forcing her to lie flat on her back with a heating pad by her side.

The first faint flutter of life sent her emotions wavering between elation and uneasiness. Comforting words from the Psalms of David were locked into her memory, and she whispered them aloud during long, pain-filled hours.

> Thou hast covered me in my mother's womb.
> I will praise thee;
> For I am fearfully and wonderfully made:
> Marvellous are thy works;
> And that my soul knoweth right well.
> My substance was not hid from thee,
> When I was made in secret, and curiously
>   wrought in the lowest parts of the earth.
> Thine eyes did see my substance, yet being
>   unperfect;
> And in thy book all my members were written,
>   which in continuance were fashioned,
> When as yet there was none of them.[1]

When their baby daughter finally was laid in her arms, a misty-eyed June traced her finger over the tiny features. Paul was as jubilant as she, and the painful months of anxiety were forgotten.

June's days were full of caring for the baby, and the experience was as wonderful as she had expected it to be. Her cup of joy was full.

When Helen Jane first smiled at her parents, her blue eyes opening wide and sparkling, Paul and June looked at each other in a spontaneous moment of wonder.

"Let's call her Janie."

And Janie she was. Janie in a ruffled handmade dress, Janie taking her first steps, Janie starting school, Janie walking home followed by her friends. It was as though God had placed a lovely rose in their home, fragile and delicate, that bloomed each year with a sweeter fragrance.

---

[1]Psalm 139:13-16 KJV

"Mommy?" Janie was cuddled in bed, looking for all the world like a pigtailed elfin, her upturned six-year-old face quizzically intent. June had just sat down on the edge of the bed to read a story to Janie, but now she closed the book and said gently, "Yes, honey?"

"Mommy, if God sees sparrows fall, why doesn't He catch them first?"

But Janie didn't wait for an answer. "My Sunday school teacher says that God sees sparrows fall; so if He does, why does He let them fall if He knows already they are going to?"

June pulled the blankets tightly about her small daughter. "Well Janie, if God lets sparrows fall—well, He just must have a reason, that's all."

"But, mommy, sparrows are so *little*."

Janie, the lover of anything small, anything hurt or helpless, the keeper of stray animals, lover of tiny fallen birds, could not understand.

"God has a reason for everything, Janie, even for fallen sparrows. We just don't always know what the reasons are."

Janie lay back and nodded. "I guess so, mommy, but sparrows are so little," she repeated wistfully. "Maybe. . ." her lip began to quiver, "maybe God will forget to watch over me."

"Janie, remember when you prayed and asked Jesus into your heart? Well, He promised to always be with you and watch over you very carefully because you are His child. God loves you just like mommy and daddy do . . . even more."

Janie was silent.

"I promise you He'll always watch over you, honey."

That night, long after the house was still, June began to send her own thoughts heavenward. "Dear Lord, watch over our baby and protect her. You gave her to us for a reason, and we unreservedly give her back to You. Lord, use her in any way You choose."

June remembered that prayer often in the following days,

and a slight apprehension tagged along behind it. Suppose God should choose to take Janie? What if that were His plan for her life? But no, that thought must be forced out of her mind. Janie was too special, a rare combination of beauty and sweetness. Still, June wished she had not used the word *unreservedly*.

Janie was everyone's best friend. The laughter of little girls playing dolls, or dreaming grown-up dreams, or calling "Come on over" filled their home. She was a blue-jeaned tomboy fishing on the lake with her dad and camping out at Big Bear Lake; she was a delicate beauty, brown curls dancing, full-skirted organdy swirling above her white patent shoes.

Paul framed a picture of small children marching into a church building and hung it in Janie's room. It was called "The Sunday School Walk"; and later when Janie would play "Sunday school" with her friends, Paul listened to her childish ten-year-old voice mimicking her own teacher, calling out memory verses for her "class" to learn. It was a moment of secret satisfaction.

Then, on a scorching afternoon in late August, June and Paul were plummeted to the depths of despair. Janie had been out playing with her friends and had come in, flushed and whimpering, "My head hurts, mom, and my neck is sore." June touched her forehead lightly and quickly drew back in alarm. Janie was burning with a fever.

It was 1952, and polio was on a rampage throughout the country. Parents anxiously watched for the slightest sign of a fever or headache, sensing that dreaded malady hovering over their children like a menacing enemy.

Now Janie lay listlessly on the sofa while June's whirling thoughts told her what must be done. She dialed the doctor's number with shaking fingers, listened intently to instructions, called the ambulance—imploring them to hurry, and quickly got through to Paul's office. The blessed relief of his strong voice brought her from the edge of hysteria.

"I'll be right home," he said.

Scenes flashed by quickly—a screaming ambulance, attendants lifting Janie while Paul and June stood by helplessly. June struggled to hold back the falling tears, taking Janie's hand just before they placed her in the ambulance. She felt a small pressure on her own hand, and Janie was whispering, "It's okay, mommy, don't cry. God must have a reason."

God must have a reason. How light-heartedly she had said those words to console her daughter when she was six. But they had been talking about sparrows, not about her precious child.

Paul drove behind the ambulance, his face deathly white. June was sobbing. The grim possibility that it might be polio, along with the solemn reality of what that could mean, gripped her mind like a tightening vise. Staccato phrases kept flashing across her thoughts—weakened muscles, paralyzed limbs, wheelchairs, iron lungs, even death.

At last they were driving into the hospital parking lot, and after Janie was placed on a stretcher and wheeled into a room, Paul left to find a phone to call family and close friends.

Nurses in starched white rolled strange-looking equipment along the shiny green-tiled floors into the examination room. They didn't even glance in June's direction, as though the weeping mother had no part in the pain of this moment.

June took a few steps down the hall, blinding tears causing her to stumble. Her Janie was lying in one of those rooms, bewildered with pain; and she, her mother, was left outside. She felt helpless and uncomforted.

A gentle arm went around her, and she turned and sobbed into Paul's shoulder, her voice muffled, "How did it happen so fast? Oh, Paul, I couldn't bear it if it is polio or if. . . ."

"June, don't you think the Lord can watch over our Janie now?"

"But what if He takes her? I told Him that she was His . . . unreservedly," she said the word in a broken voice.

Paul couldn't answer. He had never shared with June his own inner feelings that had haunted him since Janie was very small. Janie was so good, so obedient—he worried that their dream had become too perfect. It was unreasonable, he knew, but the strong foreboding kept surfacing now and again through the years. *It was the persistent thought that he would outlive his own daughter.*

He led June gently to the waiting room. When their family arrived offering their love and presence, June managed only half smiles and small bits of conversation, glancing nervously toward the emergency room at the end of the hall. And through it all she kept hearing Janie's voice whispering, "It's okay, mommy, God must have a reason."

The doctor came at last, pacing his steps as though he had walked this road many times before.

"I'm sorry," he said, not looking directly at them. "Janie has polio. She'll have to stay in the hospital." He cleared his throat, looking down at his hands. "Still, she's better off than most." His voice trailed off, and June felt pity for him. How hard it must be for him to break this news over and over to grieving parents, and how often he must have been forced to say more final, devastating words. She wanted to reach out and assure him that it was all right, that they had faith in their heavenly Father, offering some measure of comfort to the helpless doctor. But her own heart was so sore she couldn't speak.

That night after Paul was asleep, a river of tears flooded June's pillow. She was still awake when the soft light of dawn came stealing through the windows, lighting up the summer sky.

August broiled into September, and still the heat persisted. When October's amber days finally arrived, Janie's terrifying headaches, the sharp pains in her legs, and the waves of nausea had lessened, and she could begin the long road back through therapy.

The hospital had become a second home to June. At first she had carefully turned her head away from the sights and sounds of suffering in the children's ward. Her heart hammered with grief when she glimpsed little children with bandages wrapped around their heads, or tiny babies lying motionless with legs suspended high in a wire contraption, or the more frightening sight of boys and girls lying captive in giant iron lungs. June never allowed herself a second look at the iron lung section.

Janie awakened one morning to the sounds of muffled sobs from the next bed. She sat up quickly. "Hi, my name is Janie. Are you all right?"

The sobs subsided quickly, and a tousled blond head appeared over the blankets. "I'm okay."

"Well . . . what's your name?"

And the sad little girl told her, with words tumbling over each other, that her name was Becky, that her parents were missionaries far away, that she had polio and her legs hurt something awful, and that she would never ever go near that therapy room again.

June came for her daily visit and listened to her daughter comfort, advise, and *promise* Becky she would soon be well. It was an afternoon June would never forget. Watching Janie reach out with such an open heart of understanding brought a sudden rush of tears. June stood up quickly, murmuring that she would be right back, and fled the room. She walked swiftly down the hall, wanting only to be alone where she could weep without restraint. Her tears were angry and blinding. Janie should be at home playing with her friends and going to school, not confined to a hospital surrounded by pain and sickness and fear. She was only eleven, too young to see such suffering.

Someone touched her arm, and she turned. It was Miss O'Connor, Janie's favorite nurse, a smiling petite redhead who captivated children's hearts. But now her usually smiling face was sober and concerned. "Are you all right, Mrs. Grimes?"

June didn't answer. She couldn't.

"You must not weep so. You have a beautiful child. And what a help she's been in the ward, reading to the babies until they're smiling and giggling. And have you seen her with Randy, the boy in the next ward? He was so angry and depressed when he found out he'd never walk again. He played football, you know; and even though he's eighteen, little Janie's been like a mother hen with him."

June smiled wistfully through her tears, remembering Janie sitting beside the boy's bed, reading aloud to him, telling him that all things work together for good, even his illness. She recalled Randy blinking away bitter tears and nodding at Janie. "I am a Christian," he told her, "but it's hard to imagine I'll never walk again."

"Then you mustn't think of it," Janie had said firmly. She brought golden sunshine into those dark days for the young man. Miss O'Connor was still talking, and June forced herself to bring her thoughts to the present.

"You've raised a special child, you know." She patted June's arm warmly and turned to go.

June whispered a soft thank-you. It seemed so long ago that they had rushed Janie to the hospital and lived through those first hours of agony, wondering just how badly the polio had affected her. The past months had been anxious, and lately weariness had seeped into June's bones as though all strength was slipping from her body. Just then, a line from David's Twenty-third Psalm came to mind.

"He makes me lie down in green pastures." How restful that sounded now—simply to lie down and rest without cares or anxieties.

"He leads me beside the still waters." Still waters—cool, refreshing, still waters; but where, oh, where were they?

"Trust Me now, June. There are green pastures and cool waters

ahead." That sweet inner voice of her Good Shepherd filled her heart, and June whispered back, *"Where, Lord?"*

"In Me, June. Abiding in Me."

Those comforting words flooded her heart with a new sense of God's presence. In her daily rush to the hospital and her disquiet over Janie, she had almost forgotten that there was a place of perfect peace. His faithful promises, which had always been a sweet consolation to her, were once more brought to her remembrance and became dearer than ever.

"I will never fail you nor forsake you."[2]
"I will not leave you comfortless."[3]

June was serenely composed when she walked back into Janie's room, as though a soothing touch had been laid upon her soul. She picked up Janie's favorite book.

"How about if I read to you two girls?" she asked them.

When June finally placed the book down, she kissed Janie good-by then turned to Becky, leaned down, and placed a kiss on the cheek of her daugher's new friend.

It was the first good day June had had since that terrible moment in August when she had heard the monstrous word *polio.*

Life held more gleams of sunshine during October's cooling days. Becky began to relax at therapy when Janie went with her, and anyone watching the two girls splashing in the water would have thought they were at the neighborhood pool.

One day Becky's doctor walked into the therapy room when Becky and Janie were there.

"We really did it with Becky, didn't we?" he said to the attending nurse, smiling proudly. "I never thought she would be so relaxed and improve so quickly. She was so frightened at the beginning."

---

[2]Hebrews 13:5 RSV
[3]John 14:18 KJV

The nurse pointed to Janie. "Doctor, I don't think we did it at all. She did. Whatever that child did has pulled Becky through. She led that poor child away from fear."

The doctor searched for adequate words, but finding none, he smiled at the girls and left the room. It was difficult to concede, but true: medicine did not have all the answers. Sometimes the cure lay in an intangible something beyond reason and beyond science, something he could not understand.

The long days of pain were permanently engraved on the lives of Paul and June. They met parents of children who were dying. They witnessed the weariness of tired, helpless doctors, heartsick in their helplessness. They saw the nightmare of children strapped in wheelchairs, intravenous bottles attached to their arms. It was a parenthesis in their lives they didn't ever want to repeat.

"They seem so accepting . . . the children, I mean." June lay cradled in Paul's arms one night after the lights were out, and her voice was small and frightened. "They don't ever ask why."

Paul hugged her closer. "Honey, are you asking why?"

"It's hard not to. There's so much suffering. The sight of those children every day is more than I can bear. I'll never forget it. Never."

"June, I'll never forget either. But I'm glad, yes, glad that I have been able to share in some small way a part of that suffering. Honey, let's thank God right now for Janie's improvement."

"Father," Paul prayed aloud, "thank You that You have allowed us to go through this trial with our precious child. It has brought us closer to You and to others, and we thank You for that. We don't understand why it happened, but we do trust You because we know You love Janie more than we do, and we know You have a plan and purpose for her life. Thank You that she is getting better, Lord; bring glory to Your name somehow through all of this." June whispered a soft "amen," and they lay silently side by side in the darkened room.

When June finally slept that night, she dreamed of luxurious green pastures.

When October's mellow warmth bowed before November's brisk chill, Janie could come home. Paul and June drove to the hospital in high spirits. While they paid the bill and gave careful attention to instructions from Janie's doctor, Miss O'Connor settled Janie into a wheelchair and pushed her around the ward to say good-by. It wasn't easy. There was a tremulous smile on Janie's lips. These children had been her closest friends for nearly three months. They had suffered and giggled and watched hours of TV together; they had shared a special bond.

Randy, her eighteen-year-old friend, was in his wheelchair on the hospital terrace, and Janie asked to be wheeled out to say good-by to him. She playfully bumped her chair into his.

"Good-by, Randy. I hope I see you again someday."

"You're a great little kid, Janie." Randy grinned at his young friend. "And whenever I think of you, I'll remember 'All things work together for good.'"

Janie saved her last good-by for Becky. They both tried to keep the tears locked tightly behind their lashes, but Becky's wouldn't stay put. They spilled over and splashed down her pale cheeks.

"Remember, Becky, God has a reason for this." Janie touched Becky's hand, and the nurse quickly spun her around, pointing the chair toward the door. Becky was still waving after the wheelchair had disappeared around the corner, her small frame shaken by her sobs. A sweetness had invaded her life when she needed it most, and now there was just a scent of the fragrance left behind.

Paul lifted Janie gently into the back seat of their car and drew warm blankets around her thin legs.

"You okay, honey?" he asked, turning to look at her as they drove toward home. Janie was sitting quietly, looking out of the window at the passing landscape.

"Yes, daddy. I was just thinking about Becky. You see, God *did* have a reason for my getting polio. Remember, mom, you said God always has a reason? Well, Becky wouldn't go to therapy without me, and maybe she wouldn't have gotten well. So, He did have a reason, didn't He?"

Years afterward June would recall those tender words with a bittersweet remembrance, but for a long time she had no reason to think of them at all.

3

On a hot afternoon flooded with June sunshine, the seniors of Montebello High, dressed in blue and gold caps and gowns, were seated in symmetrical order on the football field. The class of 1959 was graduating.

The customarily optimistic speeches were delivered by the valedictorian and the class president; the high school band played what seemed to the spectators to be an interminably long bit of music that nobody knew; and finally the seniors filed past the principal for their diplomas. Caps were thrown high into the air, signaling the end of an era for the graduates. Hundreds of teen-agers raced for their lockers for a change of clothes and then dashed to the waiting buses which would drive them to the all-night party at nearby Disneyland.

Janie, homecoming princess

Janie Grimes had packed every conceivable activity into her high school years. She sang in the girls' glee club, marched in the drill team, acted in the senior play, cheered the teams, then like icing on the cake was crowned homecoming princess of her senior class. High school had been a perfect four years.

Janie's classic features and sparkling blue eyes that expressed inner joy drew more friends than she could number. Her home, overflowing with love, balanced her bubbling personality with a stability that was magnetic.

Just a suggestion of a limp when she was overly tired was the only physical reminder of her arduous fight with polio. Paul and June felt a sweeping satisfaction that Janie at eighteen had blossomed into a lovely young lady of unspoiled sweetness.

Janie never saw anything in the lives of her friends at school that could compare to her joy in being a follower of Jesus Christ. To Janie, being a Christian was a way of life. When others were down, she cheered them with the gift of her love. When others were lonely, she became their friend. When others needed help, she reached out and gave them the gift of herself.

Janie was no less popular in high school because she was a Christian. Her friends knew that her beliefs had made her accessible, accepting, and special.

Her classmates lauded her by autographing her yearbook with words like *loyal, sweet,* and *good*. To Janie, this was just the way a Christian should be. To be anything less would be unthinkable.

Janie in a ponytail, Janie in a formal going to the prom, or Janie in blue jeans at Curries' Malt Shoppe was the same Janie who was so admired at church. The boys circled around her, waiting to walk her home or buy her a coke, and her senior year they crowned her queen of the high school banquet.

"Mom, we're going to turn Montebello upside down for Christ," Janie had announced one evening as she was leaving to sing in a newly formed trio for a Youth for Christ meeting.

June smiled softly. Janie shared her faith in such an attractive way that June wouldn't be at all surprised if she did indeed turn Montebello and all of her world upside down for Jesus Chrst. Anyone who touched Janie's life even briefly was caught up in her dazzling smile and loving ways and never forgot her.

During Janie's last summer at home before she left for Westmont College many miles up the coast in Santa Barbara, Paul and June thoroughly enjoyed their daughter. They loved watching Janie curled up on the sofa whispering and giggling into the telephone or inviting a group of friends in for something to eat or excitedly dressing for a special date.

Paul wanted to give Janie something of himself to take to Westmont, an overflow of his gratitude to the Lord for Janie's committed life, and so he penned a song. When Janie read the words, she lifted her eyes to her father and nodded softly, "Yes, daddy, that's what I want more than anything."

> Dear Lord, I make an earnest plea
> For a closer walk with Thee.
> Take my hand, dear Lord, I pray,
> Walk with me from day to day;
> Dwell within my heart each hour,
> Fill my life with power.
> For a closer walk with Thee
> Is my heart's desire.

Janie had a hard time falling asleep the night before she left for Westmont College. She had had her heart set on Westmont for as long as she could remember, and now that the time had come, the excitement was mixed with a little apprehension. She had never been away from home for any length of time, and there was a bit of sadness in leaving her friends and the familiar surroundings of her home.

The drive to Santa Barbara on the coast highway was breath-taking. On their left the magnificent Pacific glistened to an electric blue, and on the right waving palm trees lined the road below the towering mountains. As they approached the lovely seacoast town of Santa Barbara, Janie was filled with excitement. Long winding lanes nestled between tall pines led to the beautifully situated campus.

Paul drove through the huge stone gate and parked the car. They sat for a moment gazing at the beauty. Surrounding the scattered dorms were acres and acres of green landscapes, wooden bridges, clear streams, and delightful lanes leading to as yet unexplored places.

Registration was hectic, with former and new students milling through the administration building, but finally Janie was officially signed in, had found her room in the freshman dorm, and with the help of her parents began to unpack. June felt a slight tug at her heart. Though she had tried to prepare herself mentally, it was quite a jolt to realize that her nest now would be empty, that Janie was grown and on her own.

Finally there was no further reason for Paul and June to stay, nothing more for them to do for Janie. They walked together to the car, and Janie kissed her parents lovingly, promising to write and to come home as soon as she could. She watched the blue Ford drive through the stone gates and onto the road that would lead them back to the freeway and Montebello. A new and exciting world was opening to Janie, and she turned with eagerness, ready to begin her new life.

For the past years Janie had locked a lofty dream deep within her heart. She wanted to marry a minister and walk hand in hand with him, helping the needy and ministering to the troubled. It was her heart's highest desire, and she had no question in her mind that her ideal husband-to-be was right here on this campus.

On the night of the reception for freshmen Janie wore her name tag and moved slowly through the long line of faculty, shaking hands and saying over and over, "Thank you, it's nice to be here." The large gym was decorated and filled with laughing, chatting students. The juniors and seniors were hosts to the freshmen and carried that superior look of "We've been there and we're glad we're not there any more."

"Janie Grimes? Hi! I'm Coleen, your 'big sister.'" Janie felt relief sweep through her as her "big sister" took her around, introducing her to other students.

Janie was radiant, her bubbling vivaciousness drawing new friends to her side. She was tired but almost sorry when the punch bowl was empty and the lights began to dim, signaling the end of freshman night.

"It was a fun party, don't you think?" she asked her roommate, Donna, later that night. Donna was a petite blonde from the San Fernando Valley, and they had become friends the instant they met. Donna nodded, bobby pins in her mouth, as she set her hair on large pink rollers. Janie sat on her bed, hugging her knees and thinking that Westmont was far more beautiful than her wildest dreams had ever anticipated.

The excitement of the evening had spirited the whole freshman dorm. No one could sleep, and the chatter of broken conversation floated down the hall.

Janie began scribbling on a pad near her bed.

"What are you writing, Janie?" Donna turned from the mirror.

"I'm writing a poem."

"Hey, that's great. I didn't know you wrote poetry."

Janie put the pencil to her mouth thoughtfully.

"I didn't either. I mean, this is my first one. But suddenly I want to write down something meaningful to the Lord, something I'll keep and remember always. Something to remind me of my first days at Westmont."

For Christ I'll Live

How can I tell my love for Him,
The One who took away my sin?

To love Him is to do His will;
In service, we His love instill.
Yes, He my Lord and Savior is,
The One who filled the great abyss;
I'll serve Him, yes, till life is done,
For then by Him new life's begun.
The burden's light, the road is long,
But I will follow, this my song,
To darker places than I know
Or right next door for Him I'll go.
He is my Savior, Lord, and Friend,
Without Him life would know an end.
But with Him I am safe at last
To aid in God's eternal task.

Janie tucked the poem away in her drawer and didn't think of it again for some time. Life was bright, filled with glorious new adventures. The "darker places than I know" seemed a remote possibility during those first months at Westmont.

Janie became the darling of the freshman class, double-dating with friends, exploring missions in Santa Barbara, chatting over cups of coffee, or sometimes riding down to Los Angeles for a scrumptious dinner.

One day when she was hurrying to class she spotted a young man in a wheelchair directing himself along the walk. She turned and called softly, "Randy, is that you? It's me, Janie . . . Janie Grimes."

"Janie?" Randy looked up at the laughing face and leaned back in his chair. "Well . . . Janie Grimes, we do meet again."

"And you're at Westmont. That's wonderful, Randy." Janie was genuinely pleased to see her friend from her days as a polio-stricken child at White Memorial Hospital. "Here, let me give you a hand. Where are we going?" And she began to propel the chair, merrily talking to Randy as though they had parted only yesterday.

After that Janie watched for the wheelchair whenever she

was on campus, leaving her own cluster of friends to push Randy or to sit beside his chair and talk. If she noticed that the other students ignored him, she never let on and included Randy among her choicest friends.

It was a memory that would be treasured in Randy's heart forever. His days at Westmont were difficult, but once more in his most trying times God had sent Janie Grimes into his life to be his friend. Once he told her that she didn't have to feel responsible when she saw him, and Janie's face became thoughtfully sober.

"Randy, it could have been me in that chair and you standing here. You'd do the same for me, wouldn't you?"

Randy touched her hand. "You're quite a gal, Janie Grimes."

He reminded her then of that bitter day many years before after he had learned he would never walk again, when she had repeated that treasured verse to him: "All things work together for good to them that love God." He looked down at his chair. "And, Janie," he added, "That means *all* things."

November brought cooling winds from the ocean. It was a perfect day to study, Janie thought, spreading her books around her in the large library. Just an hour or two of solitude and she could write the essay for literature that was due on Monday. She was bent intently over her papers when someone jolted her arm and whispered loudly, "Hi, Janie." It was Tommy Richardson, a boy she had dated a few times. She smiled a greeting and looked back at her paper, but Tommy was not to be put off. He sat down across from her and Janie groaned inwardly. "There goes my studying," she thought.

She had been so engrossed in her work she hadn't noticed that someone else was with Tommy—a husky, good-looking boy she had never seen around campus. He was waiting to be introduced, and Tommy said casually, "Oh, yeah, Janie, this is Gerry . . . Gerry Iverson." Obviously Tommy wanted Janie's full attention, but Gerry smiled and whispered loudly across the library table, "Hi there, sweet lady."

"Lay off, Gerry, she's my girl," Tommy said, and Janie closed her books firmly. It was a lovely day, cool and breezy, too nice to study anyway.

"Let's go for a walk," Gerry suggested, as he caught the stern eye of the librarian glancing their way.

There were three of them that day, but that was the last time. Gerry, usually so outgoing and gregarious, became the listener. He was engrossed in every word Janie spoke, and Tommy felt invisible, as though they were oblivious to his presence.

They were walking along a curved pathway on the way to Janie's dorm. Tommy had been hoping Janie would invite him to the reverse-date party that was coming up, but he could see that his chances were dwindling. Janie was smiling up at Gerry, sparkling in a way Tommy hadn't noticed before. She was obviously enamored of his friend.

Tommy swallowed a couple of times and said haltingly, "Well, I guess I'll. . . ." Gerry and Janie turned to look at him as if they were surprised he was still there.

"See you later, kids." Tommy grinned and walked away. He hadn't seen Gerry this interested in a girl for the past year and a half. Tommy had spent many melancholy moments with Gerry ever since the "Dear John" letter had arrived, breaking his engagement with Connie. Tommy knew how devastated Gerry had been since that letter had shattered his plans. He had prayed with him and listened to his sad vows: Never would he date another girl; never would he get married. No, he would serve the Lord as a single man. Never again would a girl have a chance to break his heart.

Tommy had listened along with Gerry's other friends, but no matter what they said he was lost in sadness.

"She's just not the girl for you, Gerry. God must have someone else."

"You wait and see; some gal will come along and sweep you off your feet."

But Gerry shook his head. No, it would never happen. He had loved Connie, and they had the wedding date set when she wrote that letter. For goodness' sake, didn't anyone understand a breaking heart?

Now Tommy walked back to his room with the feeling that Gerry had just met the girl who could heal his wounded emotions. *What a lucky guy,* Tommy thought, *Janie's a sweetheart.*

Those were Gerry's exact thoughts that night as he lay in bed thinking about the pretty brunette with the fascinating blue eyes, which sparkled in the most fantastic way when she smiled at him. Why hadn't he seen her around before?

"I've got a date for Saturday night," he told his roommate, Bob, "with this fabulous girl, the sweetest little gal you'd ever want to meet."

"Yeah?" Bob turned to look at Gerry. He had been through Gerry's doldrums too and had been secretly hoping he would find another girl soon. Now Gerry was lying on his back, his hands clasped behind his head.

"Well, I'm listening." Bob grinned.

"Her name is Janie Grimes."

"Go on. . . ."

"She's from Montebello."

"Yeah?"

"Well, I only talked to her for about twenty minutes. I'll let you know more after Saturday night." Gerry turned over, and Bob went back to his studies, smiling to himself. It looked as if Gerry was sliding back into love.

Saturday night in Santa Barbara was date night, and the college students were out in swarms. It wasn't unusual to bump into friends, so Gerry headed his blue VW toward the freeway and into the smaller town of Oxnard. They found a rustic-looking restaurant, and Gerry pulled into the covered entry.

They were seated in a corner booth, and the soft music set a most romantic background. The food was delicious, and the Polynesian setting was charming.

"Next time we'll go to MacDonald's, so enjoy," Gerry teased. Janie felt her heart skip at the words *next time.*

"Tell me about yourself, Gerry," she said over dessert.

"First, I want you to know that I haven't dated a girl in over a year. I . . . I was engaged. We . . . she broke off with me." Gerry had a hard time saying the words, and Janie sat quietly. "I'm sure the Lord has other plans." He glanced away, then turned back in a lighter mood. "Now . . . what would you like to know?"

"Like where you're from and why you're at Westmont, stuff like that." Janie leaned forward, her chin cupped in her hand.

"Well . . . it goes back a long way to 1937 when I was born in Glendale. I have one sister, no brothers. I went to Glendale High, hung around with a bunch of guys who are still my best buddies."

"How did you come to know the Lord?"

"Well . . . there was this guy, my best friend. His name is Don Stitzel. We went to junior high school and Glendale College together—that's a two-year college. Stitz was in Glendale for three years, and I told him he'd better leave or they'd name a building after him."

Janie laughed. "He must have loved that."

"Oh, Stitz and I are good friends. Well, back when we were in our junior year in high school, he called me one day and invited me to go to a Young Life meeting. He said, 'I'm going to stop by your house this Sunday and pick you up even if you're in your p.j.'s.' I was ready and went with him. I thought there would be a bunch of religious nuts sitting around saying weird things, but the minute we walked in I knew I'd been wrong.

43

There were about a hundred kids sitting around this gym singing, and there was so much love all around I felt good just being there. And then the speaker, Pastor Travaille, got up, and what he said really made sense to me. When he talked about the emptiness in a person's life without God, he was talking straight to me. He said we could know God personally through Jesus Christ and have forgiveness for our sins. I'll tell you the truth, Janie, from that moment I wanted to know God. I wanted Him in my life. There was no reason to wait. I just went to Pastor Travaille after the meeting and told him, 'I want what you're talking about.' He spent time talking with me, and I received Christ and was born again that night."

"How thrilling!" Janie breathed.

"All of my buddies are believers now, four of us, and we got involved in Bible studies together. I couldn't get enough of knowing what the Word of God meant. I knew my senior year I wanted to get into some kind of Christian work, so here I am at Westmont. I'd really like to go into Christian Education, training others to teach. . . . But I've talked enough about me. What about you?"

Janie told him briefly about her life in Montebello, what a happy home she had, how she had wanted to serve the Lord ever since she was a young girl. They both smiled, and Gerry laid his hand on Janie's.

"I'm glad you came to Westmont, Janie," he said softly, and Janie's heart skipped a beat.

The following Monday Gerry received an invitation in the mail from Janie, inviting him to the reverse-date party, and he sat down to write his acceptance.

November 11, 1959

Dear Janie,

After many diligent hours of intense deliberation on your proposal regarding activities of the night of the 13th of November, I have been forced to the conclusion that I would rejoice with exceeding great gladness in accepting your invitation!

At Christmas Gerry told his parents and his friends that he had found the sweetest gal in the world, and he was going to marry her. And Janie, from the night of the party, knew secretly that she was in love.

Janie had captured another heart and had sent her own into sweet captivity.

On an unusually warm December day Janie and her friend Nancy Voskuyl were decorating the window of the coffee shop, attempting to bring a bit of winter scenery into the coming Christmas holiday. They were both bubbling with effervescent chatter, animated over the coming vacation from study and exams. Their conversation centered around Christmas, their homes, and dating, and was punctuated with squeals of delight over their "work of art."

Janie had made many friends at Westmont during the past three months, but she and Nancy had become especially close. Her own spiritual life had been deepened through shared talks with Nancy, and there was a sweetness about her that was endearing. Nancy's father was president of Westmont College and, though she carried his distinctive name, she did nothing to promote it to her advantage. She was a pretty girl with close-cropped brown hair and dark eyes that danced merrily when her face broke into a smile.

Gerry had left for home a week earlier, and though tender love letters arrived daily, Janie was lonely without him. They had become inseparable, and Janie found that long hours with Gerry seemed like minutes. Now she felt lost without him on campus.

"I can hardly wait for Gerry to meet my parents and for him to introduce me to his folks," Janie was saying, and Nancy nodded with understanding.

"They'll love you, Janie." Nancy was concentrating on the top of the tree, her brush held tightly in her fingers.

"Thank goodness, Glendale and Montebello aren't that far apart," Janie laughed.

"I know what you mean, Janie. I'm . . . well, John and I are kind of that way too."

They fell silent for a time, concentrating on the last branch of the small, frosted Christmas tree. They were standing back admiring their work and didn't notice a small car that had driven around the corner until they heard the sound of its horn. It was John beckoning to Nancy, holding open the car door. She looked at Janie with a question in her eyes.

"Go ahead, Nancy. I can finish here."

It didn't take much to convince Nancy, and she ran to the car.

"Hey, Janie, come on with us. We're just going into Santa Barbara for lunch. You need a break." John was leaning out of the car window calling to Janie, but she shook her head and smiled.

"You two go ahead. I have to start packing. See you after the holidays, Nancy."

"Merry Christmas, Janie! Have a wonderful time at home. See you in 1960." Nancy's voice carried over the light breeze as she leaned out of her window, waving until the car was out of view. Janie waved back, and when she could no longer see the car, she turned back to add a few tiny stars to the decorated window.

It was midafternoon when Janie added the finishing touches to the window, but she was pleased with the wintry scene. It had taken her longer than she had anticipated, and now she would have to hurry to make it to dinner. The quiet of the campus was a bit eerie after the bustle of students; most of them had already gone home for the holidays. After dinner she would finish packing and tomorrow Gerry would be here to drive her home. She never knew a week could be so long!

A group of girls was huddled in the hall of her dorm, and as Janie walked closer she could see they weren't laughing or chatting excitedly in the usual way. They were crying. One girl was sobbing into her handkerchief, and Janie's heart began to hammer. Something was terribly wrong. The girls saw her approaching and turned, their faces solemn and wet.

"What is it?" she asked.

It was Sharon who told her. She put her arm around Janie and said softly, "Oh, Janie, it's Nancy. She's been in an accident."

Janie's mind flashed back to less than two hours before; the picture of Nancy and John waving as they drove along the curved driveway was still vivid before her eyes.

"An accident? With John?" she asked numbly.

"John is all right." Sharon began to weep now, and Janie didn't have to hear the rest. She knew.

"Nancy?"

"She's gone, Janie. Nancy's with the Lord."

The suddenness of the startling news brought a tearing sob to Janie's throat. She and Nancy had been laughing and talking together all morning. How could Nancy's young life, so filled with promise, be snuffed out so soon? *It isn't right*, she thought, *it isn't time for Nancy to die . . . it's too soon.* Her heart sent a spinning *Why?* heavenward throughout the long night.

Janie waited anxiously for Gerry the next morning, wandering around her room and bursting into tears at intervals. She wanted to feel Gerry's strong, protective arms around her. Janie struggled to control her feelings, which were plummeting to the depths of despair.

Gerry came at last, and she told him, sobbing into his shoulder.

"Honey, I know you loved Nancy. But just think—she's with the Lord," Gerry comforted, but it seemed impossible for Janie to stop weeping.

"But, Gerry, she was so young. It isn't fair to die so young. I'll never forget her leaning out of the car window, waving and laughing and wishing me a Merry Christmas," she said through her sobs.

Gerry and Janie stayed in Santa Barbara for the funeral, holding hands tightly and listening to the minister eulogize Nancy, offering words of comfort and hope.

"Because He lives, we too shall live. . . . Absent from the body, present with the Lord."

The church was filled to capacity, and Janie's spirits began to lift. The words of hope which belong to every Christian began to flood her heart, and God's peace that passes understanding filled her soul, bringing a new radiance to her eyes.

At the graveside Nancy's father and mother each put their arms around John and gently led him away. John was heartbroken—weeping like a small child.

On the drive to Montebello Janie was silent. She was thinking about John calling out to her to join them for a ride into Santa Barbara. What had held her back from putting down her brushes and running to the car with them? She could have been killed in that accident too.

With a chill she remembered another time during her senior

year in high school when a group of her friends had invited her to go to a Youth for Christ rally in Palm Springs. She had planned on going, but the flu had kept her home in bed. When the news came that an accident had claimed the lives of several of the young people, including her best friend Karen, she was inconsolable. Now death had brushed by her once more.

Now she felt the pressure of Gerry's hand on hers and said softly, "No one knows. We may have our normal life span, and then again we may have just one minute left."

Gerry nodded grimly.

Then she told Gerry about Karen, and tears flooded her eyes as she remembered. "And now Nancy . . . oh, Gerry, life is so uncertain. I could have been in those cars." Her voice was choked with emotion. "I found a verse in the Psalms last night, and I promised the Lord it would by my life verse. It says, 'Not unto us, O Lord, not unto us, but unto thy name give glory, for thy mercy, and for thy truth's sake.'"[1]

"Janie, my love," Gerry's hand tightened on her, "let's make it *our* life verse. That's my desire too—that God might receive glory as we live our lives together, not for us, but for His mercy and truth's sake."

That was a sacred moment. They would remember it again and again as the time when they had sealed their pledge to God to live in His will for His glory.

Years later in a woodsy spot on the Westmont College campus a small chapel would be built in memory of Nancy Voskuyl. On a plaque just inside the door would be these words: *Gone suddenly, where all is clear and bright.* Future generations of students would wander into the chapel to pray and meditate and wonder about the girl named Nancy, who she was and what she was like. But Janie would never forget. She placed Nancy's smiling picture in her scrapbook along with a poem, and under

---

[1]Psalm 115:1 KJV

the picture she wrote: "Nancy went home to be with our Lord near the end of 1959. Her life and death were glorifying to God and profoundly affected all who knew her."

Janie didn't know, nor could she have dreamed, that in years to come similar words would be said about herself again and again.

She may have been writing her own epitaph.

It was April 1961 and Janie's twentieth birthday. She was wearing a diamond solitaire on her left hand, Gerry's gift for her birthday; her eyes were sparkling as brilliantly as the lovely gem.

Westmont had not been the same for Janie since Gerry's graduation in December. Even though tender letters flowed back and forth daily, it wasn't enough to bridge the gap between Glendale and Santa Barbara. "This out-of-sight, out-of-mind stuff is undoubtedly the most ridiculous absurdity ever quilled," Gerry wrote. "How I love you, sweetness, and can hardly wait till we're together again."

Janie felt exactly the same way, and last spring she had broken the news to her parents. They had met Gerry at Christmas and liked him immediately, but had no idea that friendship had deepened so quickly into love. Janie was glad all of that was behind her, for she remembered the conversation well.

"Mom and dad, I have something to tell you. Gerry and I want to be married next June. You do understand, don't you?" When she saw their faces, she hurried on, "I promise I'll finish the year out and then in December, mom, you and I can plan for a June wedding." Her words tumbled out.

"Are you absolutely sure, honey?" Paul's face was both serious and tender.

"Yes, dad, I am."

"We really did want you to finish Westmont, Janie." June tried to keep her voice even.

"I know, mom, but Gerry's going to seminary this fall, and we want to be married. We want to be together." Her parents were silent, and Janie said again, "Please say you understand. Tell me we have your blessing."

"We only want what's best for you, honey. Will you promise you'll pray about it?" Paul asked.

"I . . . we have. And I'd like to pray with both of you too. I want you to know how much Gerry and I love each other and how deeply we want to serve the Lord."

They knelt down by the sofa, speaking to God from the depths of their hearts, asking Him to confirm His perfect will for Janie's life. When they stood up, they embraced tearfully.

But Janie was sure. Gerry was her love. They both were certain their hearts had found a home.

Their letters were a blend of love for each other and deep devotion to Jesus Christ. He was the center of their lives, and as their love grew they were keeping pace spiritually. They shared their daily time in the Word via the postal service. Janie saved each letter as though it were a treasure, carefully reading it over and over and writing back thoughtfully.

Gerry had introduced Janie to his parents that first Christmas, and throughout the festivities of the holidays they had come to know her and were captured by her charms. The day after Janie was back on campus a letter arrived from Gerry's mother. Janie pasted it in her scrapbook, which held cherished memories she never wanted to forget.

Dearest Janie,

First I wish to thank you for your thoughtfulness in writing to me last week. Janie, dear, may I take this opportunity to tell you how very pleased we are over Gerry's choice of a girl friend. All parents want complete happiness for their children, and when the time comes for serious choices to be made, naturally parents are very anxious that they be right from their viewpoint too. So we want you to know that we don't think Gerry could have found a sweeter, more charming, more "appropriate" girl. You just seem to be everything that he admires and respects and adores. That makes us happy. And as time goes on, I hope and believe that he will measure up to all the things that will bring you happiness too. He is a wonderful son, and I know he will be a thoughtful, kind, generous husband.

Lovingly,
Gerry's mom

Janie left Westmont in December 1960, and when the holidays were over, she and her mother began preparing for a lavish June wedding. Invitations were selected carefully; trips were made to photographers until they found just the right one; a four-tier cake was ordered; a long morning was spent at the florist pouring over pictures of flowers; and a multitude of details were attended to that June handled calmly and efficiently. Janie found the perfect bridal dress which accented her fragile loveliness; her bridesmaids had chosen and been fitted for their gowns; and now the wedding plans were complete to the last carnation. It had been a hectic, happy time of closeness for Janie and her mother, but now they were glad the preparations were over. They could relax and enjoy the next month of bridal showers and parties for Janie.

Janie's deep love for her parents burst onto paper one day in May, just weeks from her wedding. There was an envelope marked "Mom and Dad" at the breakfast table one morning, and in her concisely neat penmanship she had written:

Dear Mom and Dad,

I just thought I'd write a short note to let you know how much I love you and how grateful I am for all you have done for me. I think one of the most important and most valuable things parents can give their children is a healthy emotional outlook on life. I feel you have somehow given me this, and I thank you from the depths of my heart. I also feel it is extremely important for parents to prepare their offspring for marriage; I also feel you have done this for me. As I stand, so to speak, on the threshold of marriage about to embark on the sea of life with the one God has chosen for me, I think back over my life thus far and I feel ready with the Lord's help for this step.

I never knew it was possible to love someone so very much. Gerry is so much a part of me and I of him; I don't really feel complete or whole without him.

We don't know what lies ahead for us, but we seek to serve our Lord and Savior and to make each other happy and raise our children in the nurture of the Lord. We desire your prayers for us.

Thank you again for doing what the Lord has required of you.

With love,
Janie

Janie's letter was a legacy of love for Paul and June, one they would richly treasure at that moment and cherish infinitely more in later years.

Gerry found an apartment on North Madison in Pasadena, a walk-up that was tiny and cozy. They fell in love with it, examining each room and mentally trying to furnish it with the few pieces of furniture they were able to buy.

"It's just perfect, Gerry, honey." Janie snuggled happily next to him in the empty rooms as though it were a mansion. "We'll be together and never have to say good-by again."

Their wedding day arrived, hot and sunny. To Janie, it was the most beautiful sun, the most gorgeous sky, the loveliest day she had ever known. She hummed a line from a song on the way down to breakfast, "Happy is the bride that the sun shines on today."

June half-turned from the stove, and their eyes met. There were a lot of last-minute details to attend to before the four o'clock ceremony, but this was one last shared moment.

"I love you, mom," Janie said suddenly, and she hugged her mother affectionately.

"And I love you, Janie," June whispered. "You look positively radiant this morning. I wonder why?" She tried to laugh, but happy tears filled her eyes. It was a precious, private moment.

That afternoon Gerry and Janie stood together at the altar of the Montebello Church pledging their lifetime love and exchanging rings. Gerry didn't know until later that Janie had inscribed the reference of their life verse inside his ring: Psalm 115:1—"Not unto us, O LORD, not unto us, but unto thy name give glory, for thy mercy, and for thy truth's sake."

Later that night after the reception, after friends and family had left their home, after Gerry and Janie had changed into traveling clothes and left for their honeymoon in Apple Valley, June walked about the house turning off lights, losing herself in the joyous happenings of the day.

Pictures of Janie covered one living room wall, and June stopped a moment to gaze at them. She smiled inwardly. There was a smiling baby and there a little girl, one leg curled under her, laughing into the camera. And there was Janie in grade school, a ribbon in her short curly hair, and there again in high school wearing the look of the fifties, a cardigan sweater over a long circular skirt and a black velvet choker around her neck. There was her graduation picture, her head turned slightly over her shoulder, smiling into June's eyes. It seemed like yesterday . . . only yesterday. There on the end were pictures of Gerry and Janie laughing together on the night of their en-

Wedding day for Gerry and Janie

gagement dinner. Soon wedding pictures would be hung next to them, and perhaps someday pictures of babies again— grandchildren. June was smiling outwardly now, and Paul came up behind her and held her close. Neither spoke, for they knew each other's thoughts. It was the beginning of a new life for them, too. Janie belonged to someone else now. Their nest was truly empty.

On the edge of sleep that night June smiled into the darkness. Gerry would be a fine husband for Janie, and she would make a perfect pastor's wife. She was sure that only good and wonderful days lay ahead for them.

The only thing that was scarce in the little apartment on North Madison Street was money. Love flowed in abundance between Gerry and Janie. Gerry adored his new bride and often walked to Fuller Seminary instead of riding the bus so that he could buy Janie a card, sometimes silly, sometimes sentimental, but always with a tiny personal note in his own handwriting.

They and their friends from high school and college, Don and Nancy Stitzel, Dick and Joanne Wagner, and Don and Carole MacLane, met regularly at each other's apartments to share pizza or hamburgers or to barbecue chicken on their tiny patios.

Gerry spent his days in classes and his nights poring over his books, deeply engrossed in his study of Christian theology. His love for photography was growing into a full-time hobby. He was always the one with the camera at parties who would call out, "Hey, smile!" and snap surprised expressions, startled grins, or groups sitting at tables, forks halfway to open mouths. He had his own darkroom in the small bathroom in their apartment, and someday he hoped to have his very own developing room.

Janie worked in customer service at the gas company, as did Nancy Stitzel. They shared their lunch hours, eating peanut butter sandwiches or on a particularly affluent day a juicy piece of chicken.

When the couples were together on weekends, the four men lounged in the living room, drinking coffee and debating theological questions. The women sat with their coffee cups at the kitchen table, dreaming about the future when they would own their own homes and be able to start their families.

"It seems so far away," Janie sighed. "All I want is a baby, and I promise you by 1964 we will have one."

Gerry would graduate from seminary in 1964, and Janie pinned her dreams on that magical year.

"Honestly, Janie," Joanne said, "it doesn't seem like it will ever come true." Janie agreed.

But it did. In 1964 Gerry graduated with honors from Fuller Seminary and already had a position as Christian education director at the First Baptist Church of Canoga Park, a thriving church on the west end of the San Fernando Valley.

Janie was elated, for she was due to have their first baby in August, and now they would be able to settle in the lovely San Fernando Valley.

Gerry and Janie stood in his new office on their first day at the church, and he said quietly and reverently, "Sweetness, this is the beginning of a long and fruitful ministry."

Jeffrey was born in late August, and Gerry was able to be

with Janie through her labor and delivery, coaching her with soft assurances until the breath-taking moment when he caught his first glimpse of his firstborn. He felt an exhilaration he had never before experienced, bringing tears to his eyes.

"Thank you, Janie, my love." He leaned over her hospital bed, kissing her tenderly. "He's beautiful."

Another dream soon came true. They were able to move from their cramped apartment into a small home of their own near the church.

One day the following spring Janie was suddenly overwhelmed with the joy of her ideal life. She was sitting in the backyard while spring breezes rustled through their small elm. Jeff played happily by her side in his playpen, and she felt she must express to her parents her thankfulness in making this new home possible. She poured her gratitude onto paper:

Dear Mom and Dad,

I really feel quite silly trying to express in writing our heartfelt appreciation for your wonderful generosity in making it possible for us to buy a house. Your loving generosity makes plain to me afresh the glorious truth of God's mercy and grace to us. I do want to express to you how grateful we are for your monetary assistance; but most of all I want to thank you for being such grand parents and wonderful grandparents.

The older I get, the more aware I am of how well you did your job as parents. I know I wasn't always grateful, and I am so ashamed for the times I must have hurt you. I do love you both very much and I appreciate all that you have done and continue to do for me and my dear ones.

I only pray that Gerry and I will be as faithful to the Lord in our responsibility to our children as you have been to me.

These words are only a small attempt to express my love for you both.

Lovingly,
Janie

As always, Janie endeared herself to those who knew her, making close friends with girls her own age, as they shared baby talk and recipes and spent hours together at church gatherings or class parties while their children slept in the nursery.

It was a time of great happiness, and when two years later Gerry accepted a position at a church in Oceanside, it was hard to say good-by without tears. But by this time Janie was expecting their second child and wanted to be settled in a new home before the baby was born.

Krista Michele was an October baby, as beautifully feminine as Jeffrey was boyish.

"Janie, you do everything just right," her friends teased. "A boy, then a girl. . . ." Janie sighed happily. It did seem true. She and Gerry couldn't have wished for anything more. God had blessed them beyond all of their dreams. If they had heard somewhere that hidden blessings often came in the form of sorrow and trials, they would have agreed, but it was not for them at this time in their lives. Life was perfect, just as planned.

Krista was an adorable two when Gerry was asked to join the staff of a large church in Torrance, California.

Gerry was doing what he loved most: teaching and writing and building his photography equipment into quite a collection.

Young people began gravitating to the Iverson home for after-church socials, basking in the vitality and dedication of their youth pastor and his wife.

"It's all too good to be true, Gerry." Janie was sitting at the kitchen table, her chin cupped in her hands. "Being able to serve Jesus Christ by your side. I can't think of another thing more I could want."

"I've been meaning to tell you this, honey, but wanted to wait until it was official. I've been offered a job at Gospel Light Publications in Glendale, and I'd like to pray about it with you. You know how I love to write. It sounds ideal."

Janie reached for his hand. "Gerry, honey, whatever you

want to do is fine with me. I'm with you all the way."

They prayed together at that moment, asking their heavenly Father for guidance. When they lay in bed that night, Janie spoke into the darkness. "I have peace about Gospel Light, Gerry."

"So do I, sweetness. I just wanted to hear you say it. I'll call in the morning."

When Gerry was settled in his new position at Gospel Light Publications, they looked forward to buying a home in nearby La Crescenta, the hometown of their friends Don and Carole MacLane, and to attending the church where Gerry had found the Lord as a teen-ager.

They scouted the city for a house they could afford, but it seemed an impossibility. Then one day, when they were on their way to visit the MacLanes, they spotted a small house half-hidden by huge oak trees with a "For Sale by Owner" sign in the front yard. Gerry stopped the car. They sat quietly surveying the property until Gerry spoke. "Let's go in, honey."

When the owner answered their knock, Gerry said, "We're interested in your home, sir." Gerry knew as they toured the small, three-bedroom house that Janie was falling in love with the cozy rooms. The smile on her face was widening, and there was a "yes" look in her eyes. When they walked back to their car there was no doubt that this was to be their future home.

"Did you see that room behind the garage?" Gerry was excited. "What a darkroom it will make!"

"And so close to Don and Carole," Janie added, turning to take one last look.

They joined La Crescenta Baptist Church the Sunday after they moved into their new house. "Sweetheart, we've come home," Gerry said.

Pastor Travaille had led Gerry to Christ many years before in that very church, and Gerry had great esteem for the senior minister's leadership. Ever since graduating from seminary

Gerry's deepest desire had been to serve on the staff at La Crescenta. He and Janie had prayed for a whole year that God would make that dream a reality. While Gerry was at Gospel Light, they became deeply involved with the youth of the church, again opening their home to the college students once a week, sharing their own hopes and experiences with them and counseling and praying over their special needs.

Janie's first love had always been children, and now she began teaching fifth graders. As always, the boys and girls fell in love with pretty Mrs. Iverson's sweet, quiet ways.

Pastor Travaille began to take notice of the depth of Gerry's involvement and Janie's loyal companionship; and when there was an opening in the Christian Education Department, Gerry was offered the position. He swung Janie around their kitchen in jubilation.

"As last I feel as though this is it. We're home at our own church, and we'll never move again."

"Oh, Gerry!" was all Janie could say. After six moves in ten years it sounded like heaven to stay in one place. And what an ideal place to be—close to both parents and a short block from Don and Carole MacLane.

One day soon after their move, Janie was in her back yard raking leaves. Five-year-old Krista was near the back fence and looked up quickly when she heard a voice call, "Hello there."

It was their neighbor from the house backing up to theirs. She was standing at the fence, and next to her was a light-haired little girl about Krista's age.

"My name is Mrs. Davis, and this is my daughter, Melissa. Her nickname is Missey. What's your name?"

"Krista," she replied. "Krista Iverson." Shyly she called to Janie, "Mommy, come here."

Janie turned and walked toward the fence, setting down her rake.

"Welcome to the neighborhood! I'm Nancy Davis."

"My name is Janie, Nancy." They began to chat about the difficulties of moving into a new home, and the two little girls moved closer together, talking in halting sentences. Krista suddenly interrupted her mother. "Mommy, guess what? Missey's only four days older than me, and they go to our church."

"You do?" Janie smiled. "You're a Christian too?"

"We must get together for coffee," Nancy said.

They did, and their friendship grew through the closeness of their daughters and their mutual faith in Jesus Christ.

Janie included Nancy in her friendship with Carole MacLane, inviting Nancy to help teach in her department in Sunday school.

The swimming pool at Ron and Nancy Davis's home was open to Gerry and Janie and became a weekly gathering place, including barbecued hamburgers and iced tea and the chatter of their children. Krista and Missey became best friends, and as fall settled in, they started school together. They celebrated their sixth birthdays together, and their mutual birthday party became a yearly tradition. As one year slid into the next, Krista and Missey giggled together on the telephone every day after school, whispering, "I'll meet you at the fence," and off they would go to finish their conversation at the redwood fence.

Those were good years for Gerry and Janie, busily involved in their home and church life. There didn't seem to be anything that could possibly mar their present happiness or their expectations for all their tomorrows.

Christmas 1973 was
over. Sharply etched scenes played through Janie's mind: family dinners joyously celebrated with both sets of parents, opening presents on Christmas Eve around the glowing warmth of the fireplace, the pungent aroma of turkey cooking in the oven, the men in the family room cheering the football game on television. It seemed the happiest of all Christmases, but somehow Janie felt uneasy, almost as if there would never be a Christmas quite like this one.

New Year's Day signaled the tradition of taking down the tall tree that glittered from floor to ceiling. Jeffrey and Krista, under Janie's supervision, carefully placed the ornaments away, and at last the house was back in order. It had been a warm, serene time for Gerry and Janie. They reminisced through the holidays with continuing wonder at the ideal life God had given them. They had two beautiful children, perfect in mind and body, and above all the gift of love in Christ Jesus. He had favored them with the very best of everything.

Jeffrey at ten was the image of Gerry; Krista at eight was a miniature of Janie and promised to blossom into a rare beauty.

But now January was here, the month they had been anticipating ever since they discovered that Janie was going to have another baby. When the first symptoms of pregnancy had sent Janie hurrying to the doctor, she was not prepared for the unwelcome news. She was disappointed because she had applied for a job at a nearby elementary school and expected to begin work in the fall. But by September Janie was five months pregnant. Baby furniture had to be bought, and instead of buying clothes for work she was busy cutting patterns and sewing maternity clothes and tiny garments for an infant. Somewhere in the middle of the piled-up fabrics a secret delight stole over her. It would be fun holding a tiny baby again, and with the children away at school all day she could really enjoy this one.

That New Year's Day Janie nestled her head on Gerry's shoulder. "I've had everything," she mused. "Adoring parents, a great college experience, a precious walk with the Lord, a loving husband, two beautiful children, wonderful friends—what more could anyone ask for?"

Of course there was no guarantee that the future would be as bright as the past, but Janie had no reason to think it wouldn't be. There was no hint of shadows lurking anywhere to suggest that their life would be turned upside down in just nine days.

Janie had read every book she could find on childbirth and had carefully watched her diet so she could build the perfect baby. Gerry attended natural childbirth classes with her, and the instructor had instilled confidence that husband-coached childbirth was a beautiful, not-to-be-missed experience.

There was only one nagging doubt in her mind. During the last office visit the doctor had frowned ever so slightly when he was examining her and told her to expect an unusually small baby. Janie wondered with just a touch of fear why she would carry a small baby this time. Jeffrey and Krista had been above average in weight. Maybe it was because she was watching her weight so carefully, she thought, pushing the uneasiness to the back of her mind.

January was just into its ninth day, when Janie's first sharp pain awakened her from a deep sleep. She rolled over and looked at the clock. It was 2:00 A.M. She called out softly to Gerry, and he rolled over, mumbling. She nudged him playfully until he was alert, and from the smile on her face he knew this was the long-awaited day. They began their planned preparation, first calling Carole MacLane to come watch the children. Before the next contraction, Carole was at their door.

Janie walked into Krista's room and with loving tenderness touched her daughter's face. Her arms were flung out, and she looked so sweet and vulnerable that Janie thought how nice it would be to have another girl. But when she stood at Jeff's bed, her face softened. Jeffrey was her firstborn. He had been pure pleasure, and it would be wonderful to have another son like him. Janie stored away those precious moments in her memory. It was the last bit of clear thinking she would have for some time.

There was an early-morning chill in the air when they drove into the hospital parking lot. All of the usual formalities of signing in and informing the head nurse were taken care of before Janie was wheeled into the labor room. The doctor was on his way, Gerry told her, and then they teased each other about their natural childbirth classes. Janie wrinkled her nose at Gerry, saying, "I don't think you'll make it, sweetheart. You look awfully pale."

But there was to be no natural childbirth for Janie. The

doctor waited for signs that she could deliver naturally, but her strength was waning. "All those classes for nothing," she whispered, smiling at Gerry as she was being wheeled to the delivery room. Gerry could stay with her and see the actual moment of birth, but Janie could not deliver naturally.

The excitement in the delivery room buoyed Gerry's spirits. The doctor knew just what to do, and the white-uniformed nurses walked in and out in just the right places as though they were fitting together a puzzle. It all went so smoothly and efficiently that Gerry began to relax and watched the procedure with real interest.

It was 5:30 A.M. when Nathan Eric was born.

Janie opened her eyes and sleepily watched them lay her newborn on her tummy.

"It's a boy, honey." Gerry put his lips close to her ear. "A beautiful baby boy, and I love you, sweetness." Janie smiled and closed her eyes.

Gerry watched the nurse bathe his new son, slip a bracelet marked "Iverson" on the tiny wrist, and place him in a bassinet.

Janie was calling gently, "Be sure and tell the children they have a new baby brother."

She was asleep when she was wheeled to her room, so Gerry left to make excited phone calls. He had wanted another son, and his heart jumped when he said the words over the telephone to his parents: "It's a boy . . . we have another boy."

What Gerry didn't know was that at that very minute concerned doctors were bending over Nathan Eric, and expert hands were testing his tongue, his eyes, and his hands. With each movement more lines of worry furrowed the brows of the medical men.

Gerry was tired but jubilant when he walked into his home at 7:30 that morning and joined his children at the breakfast table.

"Well, kids, you have a beautiful baby brother." Jeffrey

shouted and Krista clapped her hands. They had both wanted a brother.

With the aroma of fresh coffee wafting through the room, Gerry realized he was hungry and gratefully ate the hearty breakfast Carole had prepared, thanking her for being the kind of friend who would crawl out of bed at two in the morning.

At the hospital Janie awakened and reached for the telephone. She felt exhausted and a little groggy, but she wanted to talk to Carole, to thank her, and tell her how happy they were. When Carole answered, Janie was effusive. "Oh, Carole, we have a beautiful baby boy!"

"I'm so happy, Janie."

"And we're going to call him Nathan Eric Thorbold."

"Thorbold?" Carole began to laugh, and Janie joined in.

"It's a family name," Janie explained, "quite a name for such a little guy." She paused.

"Carole, would you do me a favor? Would you call the girls and tell them? They're meeting at Barbara's this morning for coffee. Tell them about our baby. I'm so tired now, all I want to do is sleep."

"Of course I'll call. I'll be up to see you later, Janie. Now go to sleep."

"And oh, Carole, thank you, thank you for everything."

It was ten-thirty when Carole hung up after telling Janie's friends the good news. She had just replaced the receiver when she was startled by its sharp ringing.

It was Janie, and the moment Carole heard her voice, she felt herself go cold with sudden alarm.

"Is Gerry there, Carole? I've called his office and I've called home. I have to talk to him."

"Janie . . . Janie? What's wrong?"

Janie was sobbing, and her words were muffled.

"Three doctors were just here. They just stood by my bed and said, 'Mrs. Iverson, you know your baby is not normal.'

Just like that. They just stood there and said it." Janie's agonizing sobs brought tears to Carole's eyes. She had to say something but couldn't trust her voice to speak. Finally she was able to whisper, "What is it, Janie? What did they say?"

"They said my baby has 'Down's syndrome.'"

Carole felt a sudden chill. "Janie, what is Down's syndrome?"

"Mongoloid."

Then they both began crying, each holding the telephone tightly as though that instrument could somehow give them strength.

"Carole," Janie spoke disjointedly through her sobs, "call the girls back and tell them to pray. I'm so worried about my parents and Gerry's folks."

"Yes, Janie. I will, honey, at once, And I'll be there as soon as I can."

Carole dialed Barbara's home with shaking fingers, and her voice filled with tears while she told their friends the heartbreaking news. She knew the girls would set down their coffee cups, slip to their knees, and pray for their dear friend Janie.

At the church office the clock said eleven o'clock when Gerry sat down at his desk to open the morning mail. He wished desperately for no interruptions so that he could get back to the hospital by visiting hours. A faint smile curved his lips at the thought of Janie and their new baby, but it quickly faded when the shrill ring of the telephone interrupted his thoughts.

"This is Dr. Schafer, your pediatrician. I've just spent some time with your baby." There was a pause, and Gerry felt as though he should say something, so he murmured, "Good."

"All is not well, Mr. Iverson. Nathan is not on the critical list, but we suspect a chromosomal imbalance. We call it Down's syndrome. That is the medical term for mongolism."

The fatigue and strain of the past hours were gone. Gerry sat up alertly. *Mongoloid!* Confused, whirling pictures of strange-looking children passed through his mind, and for a moment he felt a sickening weakness. *Janie. I must get to Janie before anyone tells her.*

He laid his head on the desk after saying good-by to Dr. Schafer and tried to form a prayer, but all that came out was *Oh, God, help us; help Janie at this very moment.* He had to be calm when he told Janie, able to hold her hand and say the words gently; he had to be full of reassurance.

But Gerry knew when he walked into her room that Janie had been told. Her arms reached out to him, and they clung together, weeping as though death had taken their child.

"It can't be true, Gerry. I just don't believe it." She was sobbing in his arms.

Gerry wiped the tears from her wet cheeks. "Honey, maybe it isn't as bad as the doctors think." They clung to the hope of a mistaken diagnosis throughout the day. Carole came and sat quietly by Janie's bed, offering the gift of her friendship and love. Paul and June stood by helplessly, unable to make things right for their precious Janie.

Carole once more stepped in to care for Jeffrey and Krista so Gerry could spend the night at the hospital. He sat in a chair by Janie's bed, half-asleep with exhaustion, watching her face. She was sedated, but at intervals a sob would escape her lips until at last she fell soundly, mercifully asleep.

It was three days before Janie was allowed to see and hold Nathan. Somehow she had convinced herself that when she saw him and held him he would be perfect, and the past days would fade away like a bad dream. But when they laid Nathan in her arms, Janie's heart dropped. The longer she held him and looked down into his face, the deeper her heart sank. His eyes were slanted ever so slightly, and no amount of denial would wipe away the underlying fear that the doctors were right.

After they carried him away, Janie lay on her side, staring

out of the hospital window at the barren trees. She felt as stripped as the elm, as though a freezing wind had swept through her spirit. She lay motionless, unable to shed any more tears, letting the denial slip into a cold anger. Why had this happened to them? Why had God allowed this to happen to their baby? Or was it somehow her fault? Had she done something during her pregnancy to cause a defective child? She was still lying motionless when Gerry came, and without turning she kept repeating, "Why? Why our baby? I want our baby normal. I can't accept this. Oh, Gerry, why did God do this to us?"

Gerry didn't answer. He couldn't. His own heart was crying out the same question. He was a minister; he had been in the position of comforting others for years, but now he could not even comfort his own wife; his own heart was so troubled.

Their tranquil world had crashed in on top of them as though a giant earthquake had struck the center of their beings. They couldn't stop the shaking and tremors and aftershocks of all that Nathan's birth would mean.

It was on the fourth day, while her mother sat gently holding her hand, that Janie's anger melted into sobs of deep grief.

"Poor Jeff! Poor Krista!" she sobbed, and her mother reached out her arms to hold her. "Poor Gerry. And my poor little baby." *And poor sweet Janie,* June thought as she smoothed her daughter's dark hair, *you have just begun to grieve.*

When Gerry walked into her room that night, Janie told him firmly, "I want to be there when we tell Jeff and Krista. I want them to see Nathan and learn to love him before we tell them."

"I agree, honey."

There were two excited children in the little house on Rosemont Avenue the day Gerry and Janie came home, carrying their tiny bundle. They laid him in his crib and allowed Jeff and Krista to look at him and touch him. They stood there a long time.

"He's pretty, mommy." Krista touched his wisps of blond hair.

"I'm glad he's a boy," Jeffrey announced.

Gerry drew the children close and led them into the living room. Janie followed.

"Nathan isn't like you are," he started. He didn't want his voice to break, so he cleared his throat. "You see, God has given us a very special child, and he'll need lots of loving care. He has what is called Down's syndrome. It's kind of. . . ." Gerry couldn't say the word so Janie said it for him. "Mongoloid. Nathan is mongoloid."

The children accepted the news calmly, simply because they didn't fully comprehend the significance of what their parents had told them. They had a new baby brother and he looked beautiful to them, so whatever mongoloid was, it couldn't be too bad.

Gerry brought Nathan to Janie's bed at midnight, and she watched him closely as he struggled with the difficulty of nursing.

Somewhere in the distance a small voice was ringing through her mind. She tried to remember where she had heard the words, and when she did, tears formed and fell down her cheeks. *"God must have a reason, mommy."* It was her own voice whispering comforting words to her mother many years ago when polio had struck.

She touched Nathan's face and held him more tightly. She desperately needed consolation now, and it was her own words that God used to remind her—*God must have a reason.*

But what? Oh, what could it be? What reason could be sweeping enough to bring this cruel ache to her heart?

Through the sleepless night it was her own voice that kept recalling to her mind the moment when she had whispered those words. *"It's okay, mommy, don't cry. God must have a reason."*

Church Library
Shady Grove Baptist Church
Route One, Box 582
Carrollton, Georgia

The first two months passed like an out-of-focus dream, the kind where all the objects are rushing about with grim, unreal faces. Gerry and Janie were paralyzed with grief as though the perfect baby they had expected had died and in his place was a less-than-perfect Nathan.

Everything they read about Down's syndrome left them depressed, shaken, and filled with anxiety. Words like *feeble-minded* jumped off the pages, causing Janie to put the book down and bury her head in her arms, weeping heaving sobs. Nothing within her could accept the word *hopeless*. Nathan would be different, she told herself, but he would be as normal as she could make him if it took every minute of her life.

Their friends and families were compassionate and loving,

bringing dinner each night, speaking soft words of comfort, stopping to visit if Janie wanted to talk or simply leaving if she were overtired. Janie's slight limp became more noticeable, a sign of extreme fatigue and a reminder that once she had been stricken with polio.

Paul and June Grimes felt their own hearts breaking. It seemed the fragile rose God had given them was wilting, the petals fading and falling before their eyes.

The days were a hazy blur of sunshine passing into darkness and slipping again into dawn. Nathan slept in two-hour intervals so that Janie began to be obsessed with thoughts of sleep.

Nancy Davis filled in for her with the car pool and stopped often to offer her help. "Are you all right, Janie?" she would ask. Janie's answer at the beginning was always the same. "I'm fine, really I am." Sometimes she would break into a smile and tell Nancy how pleased they were with Nathan's progress, how far along he had come, how much more he would develop with therapy. Nancy was silent, not wishing to shatter the joyous smile of hope on Janie's face.

Later, as the weeks turned into months, Nancy would see Janie working in her backyard and call out to her, "Hi, Janie how are you feeling?" Janie would turn a drawn face and whisper, "Oh, Nancy, I'm *so* tired." *And no wonder,* Nancy thought. She herself had been up during the night and through the open windows could hear Nathan jabbering, playing with his toys, and spasmodically crying fitfully. She knew Janie was sitting in her rocker, leaning her head back, hoping for a little sleep that night.

There were welcome interludes, times when life seemed almost normal again. Carole and Nancy gave Janie a baby shower, and she was relaxed in the warmth and presence of her friends.

Janie's days were centered more and more on Nathan's well-being: enrolling him in therapy classes, working with him at home, and carrying within the seed of fear that he might contact a virus which would endanger his life.

She held him during the midnight hours, gently rocking while he was nursing, tracing his cheek with her finger and whispering, "Oh, my baby. My poor sweet angel."

Janie was grieving with an inner ache that wouldn't go away, like a constant hand in her stomach pushing her breath in and producing waves of depression and despair. She knew she was becoming irritable with Jeffrey and Krista; and though she longed to share in their everyday activities, her weariness was stealing away her usual even disposition.

"If only, Lord," she would pray, "if only Nathan were normal. I would gladly give my life." Her time of bargaining had begun, but she could think of nothing more to bargain with than her own life.

Her world had been so drastically changed, had become so incredibly marred; she could scarcely remember the light-hearted, vivacious girl she had been, the girl who had everything, the beauty queen, the sweetheart of the campus. She struggled to understand what possible reason there could be for this sudden turn of events in their lives. She couldn't even be the helpmate she wanted so desperately to be for Gerry. She was just too tired, too wrapped up in Nathan.

A thousand times a day she asked herself why she couldn't cope with her baby. After all, she was a Christian, a believer in the Word of God, and she knew that He promised that "all things work together for good to them that love [Him]."[1] And didn't He say that He wouldn't allow His children to suffer more than they could bear? Then why couldn't she get through the day without tears—tears of questioning, tears of anger, tears of grief?

And lately a deeper sense of guilt had been creeping in,

---

[1]Romans 8:28 KJV

subtly whispering that when the real test came she didn't have the faith to meet it.

She could only find relief from tension by taking a warm shower daily. She waited until Nathan was sleeping, no matter how fitfully, and slipped under the gushing water to let her tears mingle with the flood streaming down her hair and face. The hand in her stomach was tightening and she needed release, a time to weep, a time to cry out without being heard. One day she heard herself screaming and screaming, unable to stop the words that poured from her mouth. *"God, help me. I think I'm losing my mind. Oh, God, help me!"*

The shower therapy became a daily necessity to relieve the burden of depression. The screaming words bounced back against the glass enclosure. "Oh, give me strength, dear God. I'm so tired . . . so tired." The sobs were tearing at her without mercy until suddenly unbidden words crept into her mind. She heard them clearly in her thoughts over her troubled sobs. *"I can do all things through Christ who strengthens me."*[2] The water continued rushing, but the words kept tumbling into her mind like a gentle, comforting river of calm.

The tears were still flowing when she dried herself quickly and dressed, but the words were stronger now. *"I can do all things through Christ who strengthens me."* That meant staying up all night, driving Nathan to therapy five times a week, caring for Jeffrey and Krista with tender loving care, and still being Gerry's wife and lover. God promised strength for *all things*. Of course she had read and known that verse since she was a child, but now it became a life line, something to hang onto. Either it was true or it wasn't. Janie had always believed God, and she wasn't going to stop now. Then it *was* true. She *could* do all things. His Word said so.

The tension in her stomach lessened, her depression began to

---

[2]Phil. 4:13

lift slowly, and somewhere in the corners of her mind she began to hear a sweet, familiar melody. She slipped to her organ and began to play, singing the words softly:

> Some through the waters,
> Some through the flood,
> Some through the fire,
> But all through the blood;
> Some through great sorrow,
> But God gives a song,
> In the night season
> And all the day long.

Nothing had changed. The circumstances were the same—a mentally retarded child to care for, two other children with all of their daily needs, a multitude of duties as a pastor's wife—but in the midst of the unchanged circumstances God had changed Janie's heart and had given her a song in the night.

A piece of music lay on the top of her organ, and she set it before her. A smile curved her lips. It was a song her father had written some time ago, but just now it was there to reassure her that the future was as bright as the promises of God.

> Look up, look up to Him on high,
> Look to the Savior for redemption draws nigh.
> The upward look will keep your heart in tune;
> Christ the Lord is coming soon.

Of course, that was it! In the light of eternity, the afflictions she had to bear on earth were as nothing, just as the Bible said: "These troubles and sufferings of ours are, after all, quite small and won't last very long. Yet this short time of distress will result in God's richest blessing upon us forever and ever!"[3]

She could not only accept her trials but *rejoice* in them, and someday she wanted to be able to say the beautiful words of the apostle Paul and mean them from the depths of her being:

---

[3] 2 Corinthians 4:17 LB

We can rejoice too when we run into problems and trials for we know that they are good for us—they help us learn to be patient. And patience develops strength of character in us and helps us trust God more each time we use it until finally our hope and faith are strong and steady. Then, when that happens, we are able to hold our heads high no matter what happens and know that all is well, for we know how dearly God loves us, and we feel this warm love everywhere within us because God has given us the Holy Spirit to fill our hearts with his love.[4]

---

[4]Romans 5:3-5 LB

It was Thanksgiving, 1974. Janie placed a large turkey in the oven and set her pies out to cool in anticipation of the family gathering at their home later in the day.

Soon the Iversons were dressed and ready for the early morning Thanksgiving service held annually at their church. As one of the pastors, Gerry would be seated on the platform, leading in a short devotional.

During the service Pastor Travaille, the senior minister, asked those in the congregation to stand and voice any personal thanksgiving they might wish to share. Several did, but it was Janie's wavering voice that brought many to the edge of tears.

"I'd just like to take this opportunity to thank all of you who have prayed for us and for Nathan particularly this last year. I

Janie and Nathan

want to thank you for your love and support and prayers. We praise God for the way He has been working in Nathan's life and for how fantastically well Nathan is doing. God has given us the opportunity to tell other people that it is He working in Nathan's life and giving us strength one day at a time."

She sat down and met Gerry's eyes in a moment of mutual understanding. It was time for Gerry to speak, and he walked to the microphone and opened the Bible to Psalm 34:1.

" 'I will bless the LORD at all times: his praise shall continually be in my mouth.' Interesting words from the pen of David," Gerry said, "Let me refresh your memory concerning the background of this psalm.

"David was fleeing from Saul, and in a sense he went from the frying pan into the fire, because in his flight from Saul he found himself in the land of the Philistines. The Philistines were well aware of David's reputation; he had slain their champion while but a youth, and David knew he was in big trouble, so he feigned madness before the Philistine king. It is the Living Bible which says, 'Must you bring me a madman? We already have enough of them around here!' So David fled and was delivered from his enemies. Deliverance from his enemies was what caused David to write this psalm of praise.

"We have been delivered from our enemies, too, haven't we? The enemy of death, the enemy of hell, and the enemy of sin which prevents us from being our very best for Jesus Christ. We've been delivered from them.

"I want you to note David's choice. He says, *'I will.'* He could have said, 'I won't'! Through the exercise of his *will,* he assumed a particular stance in regard to his relationship to God, and he said, 'I will bless the Lord.' That is his response. Bless the Lord.

"I say that's a response because when God blesses us, we respond by blessing Him, by stating our adoration and worship and praise of Him. David continues, saying 'at all times.'

Circumstances make no difference, David said; my commitment—the choice of my will—is that I will thank and worship and adore God regardless of the circumstances.

"Well . . . how do you do that? Paul gives us the answer to that in the Book of Philippians. He says, 'Finally, brethren, whatsoever things are true, whatsoever things are honest, whatsoever things are just, whatsoever things pure, whatsoever things are lovely, whatsoever things are of good report; if there be any virtue, and if there be any praise, think on these things.'[1]

"The Living Bible translates Psalm 34:1 in this way; 'I will praise the Lord no matter what happens. I will constantly speak of his glories and grace.'"

No matter what happens. Praise in all things. The beautiful words of David's psalm kept ringing through Gerry's mind during the remainder of the service and throughout the holiday dinner while he prayed over the delicious meal and thanked God for all of His goodness to them, while he watched Nathan, now ten months old who was developing more and more characteristics of a Down's syndrome child. It was possible and it was commanded by God Himself that he, Gerry Iverson, as God's child and servant, give thanks for Nathan's illness and give praise for every single thing that came into their lives *no matter what happened.*

After their guests had gone, Gerry and Janie stood for a while in their backyard admiring the twinkling stars brightening the autumn night. His arm was around her, and he kissed her tenderly. "I'll stay up with Nathan tonight, sweetness. It's been a long day for you."

Nathan was restless, crying fitfully after the others had gone to sleep. Gerry placed him in his playpen and sat in the rocker by the window, watching the darkness deepen. He reached for his Bible and a paper fell out. It was a letter he had written

---

[1]Philippians 4:8 KJV

some time ago to his friend Fritz Ridenour at Gospel Light. Fritz had published it in their magazine, and now Gerry read it over, reliving those first weeks and months after Nathan's birth.

Dear Fritz,

We've been out of touch recently, and I got to thinking that you may not know about our new baby, Nathan. He's eight weeks old now. Let me bring you up to date. I feel I'd like for you to know the kind of "growing edge" experience Janie and I are involved in.

Later in the morning after Nathan was born, the pediatrician telephoned me at my office and dropped the bomb as gently as he could by telling me he'd spent some time with the baby.

"Good," I said.

Then he said, "All is not well—Nathan is not on the critical list, but we do suspect a chromosomal imbalance." He explained that this condition is called "Down's syndrome." I felt confused; and it didn't help when he explained that "Down's syndrome" is the medical term for mongolism.

I don't remember what else he said. I do remember thanking him as we ended the conversation . . . then wondering why. But my thoughts were with Janie. When I got to the hospital, I found she had not been told the news as diplomatically as I.

Due to a misunderstanding between the OB and another doctor, Janie's first knowledge that anything was wrong was a statement about "your child is not normal." Janie was stunned.

Fritz . . . what can a man say to his wife at such a time? I felt totally inadequate as a husband and as a minister. But God gave me the assurance that He would help me and give Janie the help and comfort that I wanted to give her so desperately.

Much of my agony was the unknown involved in the situation. I kept thinking about little Nathan. I'd seen him right after he was born, and aside from being quite blue and smaller than our other babies, he'd looked fine to me. Now I was filled with doubts . . . would he be grotesque in some way? How would he act? How would Jeff and Krista feel about a little brother who wasn't like other babies? The questions kept coming . . . faster than I could handle:

"You've given us two other bright children, God. How come You've stuck us with one who will be retarded?

"I have precious little time for my family now, God, because of being in

the minstry. Where am I going to get the extra time to give Nathan the special attention he is going to need?

"This probably will mean extra financial pressure. Where's the money going to come from, Father? You haven't exactly made me wealthy, You know."

Ironically, I had just started teaching "Why Me, God?" a course dealing with Job, to the college kids at the church. That's an interesting question when you're up against it. But instead of giving me answers, God seemed to start asking me questions.

When I demanded, "Why me, God?" I kept hearing, "Why not you, Gerry? Can you trust Me that this is for your good and My glory?"

Through the agony we managed a whispered "yes" to God, and we began to experience periods of deep peace. Nothing was really changed except our willingness to accept the situation as coming from the hand of a loving God, but that acceptance made all the difference.

With the growing peace came the ability to think back over what had happened . . . what people had said . . . how kind they had been.

Nathan was born at a denominational medical center. The chaplain had spent time with Janie. Nurses were available to pray with her, and now some of the things they said began to take meaning. For example, they had encouraged Janie to talk about her grief and muddled feelings and had tried to help her understand that much we were experiencing was the grief of loss—loss of the normal child we had looked forward to for nine months. It was like our normal baby had died and we had been given a less-than-perfect substitute.

But even as comfort and peace began to come, we kept wondering what had happened. Maybe you don't know what a "Down's syndrome" baby is, or what causes mongolism. We didn't. The doctors explained that no one knows why, but an extra chromosome occures—47 instead of 46. When this happens, there are varying degrees of mental retardation. Typically there are physical symptoms—slanted eyes, flattened bridge of the nose which gives an oriental appearance—hence the stereotype term "mongolism." There's no predicting it, no preventing it, no "cure" for it after it has occurred.

Janie and I comfort each other with our confidence that God does not make mistakes. We believe what happened to us did not happen by accident. We read from Psalm 139 that "you [God] made all the delicate, inner parts of my body, and knit them together in my mother's womb. . . . You were there while I was being formed in utter seclusion! You saw me before I was born and scheduled each day of my life before I began to breathe." We really believe that God knew about the extra chromosome all along!

Fritz, Janie and I know now by experience that when Christ said He wouldn't leave us comfortless He meant it.

Here's a kind of dramatic demonstration of how God works. We have close friends who are missionaries—one couple in Colombia and another in New Guinea. We received letters from them and also from other friends in northern California and Oregon, all within a few days of one another, telling us that they felt an unusual desire to pray for us during the few days before and after Nathan was born! They said they felt we were going through some kind of trouble or trial. Our letter to them about Nathan had confirmed their feelings.

Isn't that fantastic? Without our friends' prior knowledge of our problem, God's Spirit burdened them to hold us up in prayer. It has really helped to know that so many of our friends are praying for us and Nathan.

Now about Nathan himself. He really is a lovable little guy. He's a good baby and, so far, is very much like our other children were at his age. He eats well, sleeps better, and is gaining weight now. What really pleases me is the way he smiles and responds to us.

Through some interesting circumstances Nathan has become part of a research program at the Regional Center for Mental Retardation. The head doctor says that at this point he isn't a very good candidate because he seems to be doing so well.

After these first rough weeks Janie and I are truly grateful for our special little boy who has captured such a special place in our hearts. Jeff and Krista are enjoying their roles of being big brother and sister. They know Nathan is different, but they love him and accept him as a special little brother.

Janie's attitude toward the whole situation has really been helpful to me. She has expressed on several occasions that Nathan's arrival in our lives has resulted in God's showing His faithfulness and love through His body, our brothers and sisters in Christ, in a fuller way than we've ever known. Nathan has brought us so much joy and love that we can't imagine our family without him!

> *Your brother in Christ,*
> *Gerry*[2]

[2]Reprinted from *Family Life Today*, © 1975 by G/L Publications, Glendale, CA 91204. All rights reserved. Used by permission.

Jeffrey, Krista, and Nathan

You know, Mrs. Iverson, the Lord can heal your son Nathan." The voice on the other end of the telephone was firm and decisive.

Janie had just come home from a day with Nathan's therapist and was tired to the bone, longing for one hour of sleep to turn off the wheels of her mind, to shut out for a time the doctor's list of what must be done daily for Nathan, what he must eat, and that he must eat whether he felt like it or not. It was all spinning through her mind on the drive home. Nathan was restless and began to cry long and loud on the last miles along the bumper-to-bumper freeway. Janie had to steel herself to keep the car steady and talk in soothing tones to her exhausted baby. Now he was in his crib and had thankfully fallen asleep when the sharp ringing of the telephone had stopped her abruptly. *Oh, please not now,* she thought. *I'm too tired to talk, too weary to think.* But she was Mrs. Gerry Iverson, pastor's wife, and might be needed. The voice on the other end of the line talking about Nathan's healing sent her senses reeling.

"Who is this calling, please?" she asked politely, although she was sure there was a bit of ice in her voice. *God,* she prayed inwardly, *this is the thousandeth time I've heard this. Please give me patience. Don't let me be angry.*

"This is Mrs. Barton. You don't know me, but our church has been praying for little Nathan."

"Thank you," Janie said. "I . . . we . . . Gerry and I appreciate that."

"But you can't settle for his illness, Mrs. Iverson. We know that God is able to heal. You just need more faith—"

"Mrs. Barton," Janie purposely kept her voice low, "we do know God can heal, and we feel He can heal Nathan any time He wishes. . . ."

"Why don't we come to your home and pray with you and your husband? We would like to lay hands on Nathan and pray for his healing. The Lord has given us a word, and we believe that Nathan will be healed."

Oh, dear God! Janie's mind was spinning. What did this strange woman who had never set foot in their home know about Nathan? Did she know the anguish in their hearts, the crying out to God to heal their precious son? Did she have any inkling of the hours they had held him and in faith believed God for his complete wholeness? They had submitted to every truth in God's Word, believing with trusting faith, but Gerry had admonished her that God often has a purpose in illness and affliction, and together they had trusted God for whatever He chose to do in Nathan's life.

"God will heal our baby in His own way and time. It may not be on this earth, honey," Gerry had told her, "and if it is not to be on this earth, He will give us grace to bear it."

Janie thought of the times she was alone in the house just after Nathan's birth when she had screamed out to God to help her and how the verse that God had given her slipped into her mind: "I can do all things through Christ who strengthens me." She remembered the exact day of her complete yieldedness to God's perfect will and the peace that had enveloped her ever since.

Now Mrs. Barton's voice was cutting into her thoughts. "Would it be all right if we came to your house to pray for Nathan?"

There was a long silence, so Mrs. Barton went on.

"You know healing is in the Atonement. In Isaiah 53 it says, 'By his stripes we are healed.' It's an accomplished fact. All we have to do is claim it."

Janie wearily passed her hand over her forehead.

"Mrs. Barton," she had to bring this conversation to a close, "Gerry and I do have faith in our loving Father. We do believe. We have had hundreds of people praying for Nathan. But now we have an acceptance in our hearts that God has a plan we cannot know or understand."

"You can't settle for that, Mrs. Iverson. God is able to cast out any demon of illness."

Janie winced. The words brought quick tears to her eyes. Her precious little baby, her special child sent for God's own purposes, had become the means of many hours of consoling others who needed comfort. Because of her trial she had a new understanding of those who were going through deep waters.

Now she turned her attention back to the caller on the other end of the wire. "I really want to thank you for calling and showing concern for our son, Mrs. Barton; but when you do pray for Nathan, as I hope you will, could you please pray that God will receive glory in any way He chooses? And please pray for Gerry and me that we might rejoice in tribulation; that I as

Nathan's mother may continue to comfort other mothers whose children are born with Down's syndrome; that somehow through this I may be able to show them that our light affliction is but for a moment and what we are suffering now is nothing compared to the glory that is awaiting us; that I may show others the love and grace of our Lord Jesus Christ so they might come to know Him as Savior."

When Mrs. Barton answered she simply said a short "We will continue to pray for you."

Janie replaced the receiver thoughtfully. While she had been asking for that needed prayer, a new calm had steadied her, renewing her strength. Today had been heavy and filled with burdens, and she had almost forgotten the gentle words of her Savior: "Come to me, all who labor and are heavy laden, and I will give you rest. Take my yoke upon you, and learn from me; for I am gentle and lowly in heart, and you will find rest for your souls. For my yoke is easy, and my burden is light."[1]

His burden was light. She didn't have to carry the load alone. Her heart was full of speechless gratitude.

She had prayed some time ago that God would use her in any way He could to comfort others, and she made a new affirmation of that promise at that moment. She would no longer wait for the opportunities to come to her. She would notify the doctor to call her if any other mother ever had to hear the words *Down's syndrome,* and she would go directly to help her in the first moments of grief and to comfort in any way she could.

It was a promise she kept faithfully to the end.

---

[1]Matthew 11:28-30 RSV

Gerry?" The voice on the other end of the telephone was Dr. Schafer, Nathan's pediatrician, and Gerry wondered with alarm why he was calling him at the church office. "Gerry ... I ... we have another Down's syndrome baby, and the mother is in a deep depression. I thought maybe you could call on her. Perhaps knowing you went through what she is facing might be of some help."

Gerry's heart dropped. It was almost as though he were hearing the words *Down's syndrome* for the first time. He knew he could offer sympathy and understanding, but his own wounds were so fresh and hurting it would be like opening them to more pain than he could bear. Still, he was a servant of Christ; he longed to serve Him with all of his heart; he had given his life to minister to others. How could he fall short when his help was needed so desperately?

"Her name is Pam . . . Pam Nelson," the doctor was saying. "Gerry, I think you'll understand that she is very hostile now, but we're hoping you can break through that hostility and help her."

Gerry glanced at his full calendar, mentally canceling his afternoon engagements, and thought back to the day when Dr. Schafer had called to break the news about Nathan. Though he felt now that he had accepted Nathan's affliction, he couldn't deny the pain in his heart nor the feeling that it would always be there. He and Janie had prayed together often, promising God that they would trust Him even when they could not understand, that their life verse was still in their hearts—to bring glory to God. He knew part of serving the Lord was sharing in others' sufferings and sharing his own suffering with others. He opened his Bible and sat thoughtfully and quietly reading 2 Corinthians, letting the words sink into his mind.

> What a wonderful God we have—he is the Father of our Lord Jesus Christ, the source of every mercy, and the one who so wonderfully comforts and strengthens us in our hardships and trials. And why does he do this? So that when others are troubled, needing our sympathy and encouragement, we can pass on to them this same help and comfort God has given us. You can be sure that the more we undergo sufferings for Christ, the more he will shower us with his comfort and encouragement. . . . In our trouble God had comforted us—and this, too, to help you: to show you from our personal experience how God will tenderly comfort you when you undergo these same sufferings. He will give you the strength to endure.[1]

After the words were written on his heart, he asked his secretary to cancel his appointments, walked out into the cool November afternoon, and drove his Renault through the streets

---

[1] 2 Corinthians 1:3-7 LB

of La Crescenta to the large hospital on the edge of town.

There was no doubt that Pam Nelson needed comforting. Her blue eyes were dark with rage and pain. She glanced at Gerry and quickly looked away.

"You're a preacher, aren't you?"

"Yes, I am, Mrs. Nelson," Gerry answered. "Dr. Schafer asked me to come. I'd like to talk to you a few minutes."

The hostility in the turn of her shoulders was so apparent that Gerry found it hard to form words. He could only say, "I understand. Believe me, I understand."

She turned then, fiercely, her eyes glaring into his.

"*You* understand? You *understand?*" Her voice was gathering momentum and was on the edge of breaking into sobs. Gerry could feel his own tears gathering. "How could *you* understand? How could you know what it means to hear those terrible words, 'You have a mongoloid baby'?" She was sobbing into her hands, her head turned as though she were ashamed to look at Gerry, as though there were some stigma attached to her.

"Mrs. Nelson . . . Pam," Gerry said evenly, "we *do* have a mongoloid baby."

The sobbing stopped suddenly, and she turned her head in sharp unbelief. She looked at Gerry, and her hands came away from her face. It was the first moment she had felt anything other than raw and savage pain. She knew there were other Down's syndrome children somewhere, in a home maybe, but she didn't know any. And none of her friends had ever heard of anyone having a mongloid child. Now this good-looking young minister was telling her that he did understand because right in his home was a baby like hers.

"Our little boy Nathan was born in January. He's ten months old now, awfully cute and lovable." She didn't say anything, so Gerry went on. "I was just standing at the nursery window, and I asked to see your baby girl. I want to tell you, I got excited, because she had lots of muscle tone, more than Nathan. You should be thankful."

"Thankful?" her voice rose again in tears. "Thankful for a mongoloid child?"

"Pam, let me tell you a little of how my wife, Janie, and I felt when we first heard the news." He leaned against the foot of the bed and relived those first terrible days. "Let me name our feelings and perhaps you will recognize you own feelings now. We felt guilt . . . yes, guilt . . . thinking that somehow *we* may have been responsible in some way. Maybe we did something to cause this affliction. Then we began to deny that anything was wrong with Nathan. We thought the doctors had simply made an error in judgment and that it would be corrected in a few days. It didn't seem possible that *we* could have a mongoloid child. Then denial lit the flames of anger, and they were all directed at God. Remember, we have trusted God and are serving Him, and yet . . . and yet . . . we were screaming out, 'Why us, God? Why our son? What purpose could there possibly be for this to happen to us?' And after the anger subsided, there was a tremendous disappointment, as though the baby we were expecting had died and in his place was this baby that we neither expected nor wanted."

Pam's eyes were brimming with tears. This young minister *did* understand and had captured the feelings which had been raging within her ever since the birth of her second daughter, Shelley. When her husband, Larry, had stood at her bed and told her the news, weeping in a heartbreaking way, feelings of denial, anger, guilt, and disappointment had tipped her emotions like gigantic waves until she felt she could no longer swim against the tremendous undertow of her feelings.

"I'd like to pray for you, Pam, and then come back tomorrow." Gerry didn't wait for an answer but began to talk to God. It wasn't like any prayer Pam Nelson had ever heard. It wasn't flowery or lengthy and didn't sound like a minister at all. He was actually talking to God as though He were in this room with them. He was asking for strength for her and her husband and peace in the days to come. Before he left, he asked if he could bring Janie and Nathan to their home. "We want you to see Nathan, to see how sweet he is and how much progress he has made."

Pam nodded. Shelley would have to stay in the hospital for two more weeks, she told him, but after that she would like to meet Janie and Nathan. When Gerry walked out of the room, Pam felt as though a weight had lifted from her heart. There was someone to talk to, someone who would understand, and someone who knew how to pray. She was crying softly, but along with the sadness there was a new comfort that lulled her gently to sleep.

When Pam met Janie a month later, she looked into smiling blue eyes and thought immediately, *What a sweet person!* There were no signs of anger or bitterness. Janie bubbled with excitement as she set Nathan on the floor and showed Pam what he had learned at therapy.

"I'm really enthused about therapy and this school Nathan is attending. I know you will be, too, Pam, and we could drive together. It would be great to go with someone."

The Atwater Park Center for disabled children was located in the heart of Los Angeles, and there mothers of Down's syndrome children filled the therapy rooms. They were encouraged to work with their children at home and were taught how to help them develop and progress. There was an immediate bond between the mothers who had suffered through the same times of despair; theirs was an understanding that did not have to be formed into words. Pam enrolled Shelley in the school and together with Janie and Nathan made the long drive to Los Angeles five times a week.

In the months that followed, Janie became more involved, more caring about children other than Nathan and volunteered to help while Nathan was in therapy. She fed other children, changed them, played with them, read to them, and hugged them as though they were her own. Pam thought how hard it would be to take care of someone else's mentally retarded child. It was hard enough accepting Shelley; and, though she never told anyone, she had secret doubts that she even loved her.

Shelley's birth had caused tension in her marriage, and as she watched Gerry and Janie so obviously in love, she wondered what it was that could help them survive something like this.

During one of their frequent trips to therapy with their children, Pam turned to Janie and asked intently, "Janie, what is it that's different about you and Gerry? What makes your marriage work?"

Janie was thoughtful for a moment. "Pam, it's because marriage is a triangle, or at least should be. God is at the top and the husband and wife at the base. It's our mutual trust and obedience to *Him* that makes our marriage what He intended it to be."

Pam sighed. "You make it sound so simple," she said wistfully. She was thinking of her own floundering marriage.

"It's a matter of total commitment," Janie said quietly. "Unless we are willing to commit our lives to Jesus Christ, we are really not ready to commit our lives to another human being. That *must* be the first step."

Pam didn't answer. She was holding Shelley closely on her lap and keeping one eye on Nathan strapped into his car seat.

"Pam," Janie said gently, "you and Larry are not two perfect people. Neither are Gerry and I. But with God at the head we can rely on *His* strength, *His* forgiveness when we fail . . . and we do."

"You talk about God as though you know Him personally . . . as though He were your best friend. To me He's just been an idea . . . a concept of someone way out there . . . not too involved in our lives."

"I think I know how you must feel, Pam. But we can know God through His Word, the Bible, and when we read there how much He loves us, how personal He really is, it's hard not to respond to that love."

Pam wanted to ask Janie how she could have faith in a God who would allow handicapped children to be born, but she was silent on the rest of the drive that day.

Janie had something special she knew, and Pam found herself depending more and more on her for strength and comfort, often calling her for long conversations, unburdening her heart.

Janie remained calm and unhurried, listening with understanding. Whenever she asked Janie if she were busy, the answer was always the same, "Yes, I'm busy, but I'll sit down awhile. The rest will be good for me."

One day Janie stopped at Pam's for coffee, and as they sat across from each other, Pam confided, "Janie, I have something to tell you."

Janie waited.

"I found out I love my baby! I mean I didn't know if I really loved Shelley, but I know now that I do. It happened in a funny way. I had Shelley in the infant seat, which was clamped to a kitchen chair. I was scrubbing the floor, and when I pushed the chair out of the way, Shelley fell! She fell right onto the floor and bumped her head, and . . ." Pam began to weep, and Janie bit her own lip to keep from crying. "I knew in that moment that I loved Shelley. I picked her up and held her close and kept crying, 'Oh, my precious baby, I love you and wouldn't do anything to hurt you!'" Pam was sobbing now, her face buried in her hands. "Janie, I wondered if I was trying to kill my own baby, and when I held her close and kept saying the words, 'I love you. Mommy loves you,' Shelley stopped crying; and, Janie, she smiled at me. It was the first time she ever smiled. I knew that Shelley knew I loved her, and what a change has come over her.''

They were both crying now, as Pam's deepest feelings flowed from her heart. "I questioned whether there was a God if He would allow this child to be born; but I know now through you, Janie, that there is a God and there is some reason why this happened to me.''

"God always has a reason, Pam," Janie said softly. She took a letter from her purse and handed it to Pam. "I want you to read this letter from a dear friend of mine. It has helped me so much.''

Pam read it, and when she came to the last lines she read them aloud. "Now remember, your baby is just like any other baby. Enjoy him because he's soft, sweet, cuddly, and loving.''

"I have something else for you, Pam." Janie handed Pam a folded piece of paper. "It's a poem I've copied for you. I keep it in my kitchen on the bulletin board where I can see it every day.''

Pam didn't look at the paper. She laid it down beside her coffee cup. "Let me read it later, okay?''

Janie nodded, understanding that Pam's emotions had been stretched to their limits that day.

The bond between Janie and Pam had begun because of Nathan and Shelley, but now Pam had grown to love Janie just for herself. She had never known anyone so loving, so giving, so unselfish. She told her so one day.

"It's because of Jesus," Janie said simply.

Pam grew uncomfortable. "But, Janie, you're just a sweet person.''

"If I am, it's because of the love of God He puts in my heart.''

"The love of God." Pam looked out of the window at the ripple of cool, blue water in her Olympic-size pool. "The love of God," she repeated as though she could not grasp the thought. God and love seemed to be synonymous to Janie.

"His love is unconditional, Pam. He loves us no matter what happens. And if we love Him, we must love others. We do that by letting His love flow through us."

"Sounds kind of mystical, Janie—not at all like the real world."

Janie smiled, pulled a small edition of the Living Bible from her purse, and turned the pages quickly. She handed the Bible to Pam. "I'd like to leave this with you, Pam, and tonight when you are alone, read these words." She pointed to one section. "That is the way we should love. I'm afraid I fall far short of that."

Pam kept the Bible open, and that night after Shelley was asleep, she found the words Janie had pointed out. She didn't care that Larry might walk in and wonder why she was reading the Bible and perhaps make disparaging remarks. The words held her spellbound. She said them aloud softly.

> Love is very patient and kind, never jealous or envious, never boastful or proud, never haughty or selfish or rude. Love does not demand its own way. It is not irritable or touchy. It does not hold grudges and will hardly even notice when others do it wrong. It is never glad about injustice, but rejoices whenever truth wins out. If you love someone you will be loyal to him no matter what the cost. You will always believe in him, always expect the best of him, and always stand your ground in defending him.[2]

If anyone in this world were even close to that ideal, Pam thought closing the Bible, it was Janie Iverson. Those words could have been written about Janie.

Winter, summer, fall, and spring rolled around once, then twice. Janie and Pam drove the freeways together during that time, taking their children to the Atwater School for therapy. Nathan was progressing at a rate that surprised even his ther-

---

[2] 1 Corinthians 13:4-7 LB

apist, and Pam felt her own heart encouraged at the way Shelley was responding to therapy.

On a hot July day that made the drive home from the inner city school seem endless, Janie rolled to a stop in front of Pam's ranch-style home.

"I won't see you until the last week of August, Pam," Janie said. "I'm going to Big Bear Lake next week with my friend Carole, and the following week our family is going to vacation there."

Pam suddenly noticed how tired Janie looked. Dark circles had formed around her eyes, and weariness seemed to steal away the rosy glow from her cheeks.

"I'll miss you, Janie," Pam said as she lifted Shelley from the back seat.

"Oh, I'll call when I get back. I'm looking forward to the rest and just being alone with my family." Janie leaned over and kissed Shelley on the cheek. Then she turned to Pam with a serious look on her face. "Pam, I want you to know that I have finally made the adjustment to Nathan, and now I am ready for whatever God has for us in the future."

Pam felt a sudden uneasiness. It was almost like a final good-by. She smiled and waved until the white Renault disappeared around the corner and out of her life . . . forever.

It was the first week of August. A shimmering heat beat down on the city, making each day hotter than the one before, and the dry Santa Ana winds whipping around the tree-lined avenues only intensified it.

At high noon on Monday Carole MacLane's station wagon rolled away from the city of La Crescenta heading straight for the mountains and their cabin at Big Bear Lake.

The three MacLane children sat in the back seat, while Jeffrey and Janie, with Nathan on her lap, were in front with Carole. The soft whirring noise of the air conditioner was a blessed relief after the blast of hot air from out doors.

It was the first time in their fifteen years of marriage that Gerry and Janie had been apart even for a week, and it had taken some persuading on Janie's part to convince Gerry that she would be fine . . . that she and Carole needed to prepare the cabin for their vacation the following week. And, yes, he could call her whenever he wished. She would be back home on Friday night, and he should check on Krista, who was staying with Missey.

The two-bedroom cabin had a large living room with an elaborate stone fireplace, the one luxury Don MacLane had insisted on when he had it built. A kitchen complete with modern conveniences included a large round table that could easily seat eight.

The beauty of the shimmering lake, the pine-covered mountains in the distance, the uneven terrain covered with pine cones, and the fresh, clear air sent the children running for the lakeshore.

Carole and Janie sighed happily while they opened windows to let in the cooling breezes and put away their luggage and groceries. It was hard to believe that they had left such intense heat back in the city; but now they were here for five days, away from everyday chores, errands, and even television sets.

Nathan restlessly scooted around the cabin, pivoting this way and that, racing back for Janie's lap. She lifted him gently each time and held him close; he had almost become an extension of herself.

Carole had never lived on an hour-by-hour, day-by-day basis with Nathan before, and suddenly she could see how demanding life with him could be. No wonder Janie's face had become drawn and dark circles had painted their way around her eyes, robbing her of the sparkle that had once lit up her whole personality. Carole had witnessed a vivacious girl transformed into a mature, thoughtful woman. Now she could see why. Nathan took every bit of Janie's time, every ounce of her energy. Carole resolved to make this week as easy for Janie as she could. Somehow, some way, she was going to put that twinkle back in Janie's eyes.

She caught Nathan to her and called to Janie, "I'm taking Nathan for a walk. Why don't you just freshen up and rest awhile?" And she was gone before Janie could protest.

Janie leaned back in the rocker and rocked slowly back and forth. The stillness around her was a luxury she hadn't known for some time. A cool breeze wafted through the kitchen window and played through her curls.

It was not the days with Nathan she minded, although they were tiring and she had to watch him every minute. It was when darkness fell that her spirits sank. Nathan couldn't sleep for more than two hours at a time; and when he finally did, his sleep was so fitful that Janie felt and heard every outcry. Her sleep had become as spasmodic as his, wearily trying to awaken herself at his insistent calls, forcing herself to walk to his crib, change him, lift him out, and let him run through the house. The night had become an intimate friend; she knew every sound each hour would bring and the exact moment that dawn would come creeping through the windows. The night became one long prayer for just a little uninterrupted sleep.

Now Janie was thinking back to an interview she had given the local paper. It was hard to tell anyone, especially a stranger how she felt about caring for a baby with Down's syndrome. She couldn't explain the thousand surging feelings or describe the pent-up emotions of joy and sorrow—joy when Nathan made one step of improvement, sorrow when she remembered that he was different. She had tried to say what was in her heart and wondered if it had made any sense to the interviewer. She remembered now one line of hers that he had quoted: "I don't know what is in store for my children or for me and my husband. But the Lord has promised to give me strength for one day at a time. Now that I believe that, I have such peace."

Janie smiled to herself. One day at a time . . . that had been the secret after all—living out each day as it happened and letting the future rest in God's hands. She had to call her mind back many times from the distant, unknown future when Nathan would be grown and in high school, or imaginings of something happening to Gerry, or a thousand things that popped into her thoughts. She knew peace through day-by-day thinking.

The week went slowly and became more restful and lovely each day. Janie's insatiable zest for reading could be satisfied this week with someone to watch Nathan; and so hour after hour she sat motionless, her feet curled under her, lost in another world.

Every morning when the mist cleared away, the older children ran for the village or the lake while Carole and Janie sat together chatting quietly. They planned to the last detail the fortieth wedding anniversary celebration for Janie's parents the following Sunday.

"I want it to be perfect." Janie glanced guiltily at the fabric they had brought to make her a dress for the party. But Carole interruped her thoughts.

"Janie, just rest this week. You can wear my long beige dress; it looks lovely on you."

Janie sighed in agreement. It would be more fun just to rest and talk and read.

Carole and Janie had both resolved to lose four pounds before the week was over, and laughingly they watched each other carefully. Every night after dinner they all walked to the village store, and when the children ordered ice cream, Janie and Carole shook their heads, "Not even a bite . . . not one."

One day Carole told Janie that she would stay up with Nathan that night; Janie was to *sleep*. The thought of one night without worry or interruption made Janie quickly agree.

Throughout the night, Carole saw what life had become for Janie. Nathan was wide-awake; he needed changing; he wanted to run through the cabin and there was no holding him back. The darkness seemed blacker in the mountains under towering trees; each shadow was threatening. It was a night Carole would never forget. But the next morning when Janie awakened with a new sparkle in her eyes, it was reward enough for Carole.

"Carole, that's one of the few nights I have slept through since Nathan was born. How can I ever thank you?" They sat together at the breakfast table holding cups of coffee when suddenly Janie set hers down. "Carole, I know I should thank God *in* everything and *for* everything. I'm at the '*in* everything' place but not the '*for* everything.' I can thank God *in* these circumstances that He will work everything out for our good, but it is still impossible for me to thank God *for* Nathan's affliction. Perhaps that will come." Her voice trailed off softly.

Carole reached for her Bible and turned quickly to 1 Thessalonians 5:18: "Give thanks in all circumstances; for this is the will of God in Christ Jesus for you." She looked up.

"But here it says *in* everything, Janie."

"I know. But it's Ephesians 5:20 where Paul commands us to gave thanks *for* all things."

Carole looked it up and read it aloud thoughtfully. "Always and *for* everything giving thanks in the name of our Lord Jesus Christ to God the Father."

They were silent, each thinking of the awesome possiblity of giving thanks *for everything*.

"I hope to get to that place, Carole," Janie said finally, "where I can thank God for everything, including Nathan's Down's syndrome, my lack of sleep—everything."

"That's quite an assignment, Janie," Carole almost whispered. "Easy when everything is going well but, wow . . . when things aren't. . . ."

Carole thought a little guiltily of how wonderful her own life was. It was easy for her to give thanks, for she had an adoring husband and healthy, loving children. How would she react if suddenly an upheaval came to change the course of her world?

Carole didn't know the answer, and later on how thankful she was that she didn't know that such an upset was on the way and that she would remember Janie's soft voice whispering about giving thanks . . . and that Carole herself would cry out with all of her strength for the courage to give thanks *in* and *for* all things.

Missey!'' The tele-
phone rang for what seemed like the hundredth time on Satur-
day morning, and Nancy Davis called her small daughter
rather impatiently. "It's Krista!" she called and turned back to
folding clothes.

It was a bright August day and their pool looked coolly
inviting. Nancy folded the last towel, patted the pile in a final
gesture of relief, and went to change into her swimsuit for a
quick dip and a nap in the sun. She wanted a deep tan and
today was just perfect. The sun was high and hot.

She heard Missey whispering into the phone, "I'll meet you
at the fence," and replace the receiver noisily in its cradle. She
winced as Missey raced by her and out the back door.

Nancy lay back on the lounge and longed for one hour of

Photograph of Krista taken by Gerry at the
anniversary party

solitude. She closed her eyes, thinking she might have the luxury of a few minutes of sleep, when ten-year-old voices floated past the fence and over the pool to her ears.

Krista was leaning across the fence breathlessly.

"Missey, something awful happened! Remember my friend, Suzanna? Well . . . she went to camp and went swimming and—" Krista's voice dropped as she caught her breath—"she drowned! Oh, Missey, she drowned!"

Missey was wide-eyed. "How terrible! You mean she really *died?*"

Krista nodded. "I could hardly believe it when my mom told me." They stood in silence for a few moments.

"I really loved her." Krista's voice was fading.

Missey reached over and touched her hand lightly.

"I'm sorry, Krista."

"I'd sure hate to die," Krista said slowly, cupping her chin in her hands and looking up at the blue sky. Missey nodded in agreement. They couldn't imagine someone being alive, laughing and playing on earth, and then suddenly being gone forever. It was too awesome and disquieting to even comprehend.

"I guess everyone who loved me would miss me too," Krista said, and Missey nodded. Suddenly she brightened.

"But, Krista, just think—if we died we'd be in heaven with Jesus."

They fell silent, and Nancy listening to the two little girls deep in conversation about death, felt hot tears stinging her lashes. There was an aura of tenderness in that moment as she sat in stillness beside her pool.

Krista said finally, "Yeah, I know I'd be with Jesus, but just think how my family would feel. Missey, when I die, I want to die with my whole family and be buried next to them."

"Wow!" Missey was startled at the thought but decided it was too absurd an idea to pursue, so she said thoughtfully,

"Krista, do you think it hurt Suzanna? I mean, I wonder if it hurts to die."

"Yeah, I wonder too. I hope when I die it won't be in a painful way."

"Well, I don't think God would let it hurt too much, Krista. He loves us too much to let it hurt terribly, don't you think?" Her voice was uncertain.

Krista smiled suddenly. She had made Missey feel sad, and now she wanted to say something happy.

"Wouldn't it be fun to visit heaven just one hour a day? I'd like to see what it's like and then come back and tell Suzanna's mom and dad and brothers all about it and how happy she is there."

"Yeah." Missey looked far up into the blue heavens. "It would be fun to visit heaven once in awhile, but we can't see heaven till we die or till Jesus comes back."

Krista's face lit up and she giggled. "I know this sounds silly, Missey, but if I am still alive when Jesus comes, I want to hang on to my pets when I float up to meet Him 'cause I want them to go to heaven too." They laughed together self-consciously.

Nancy wanted to go to the girls, hold them close, and tell them they were very young, that they wouldn't die for a very long time, that it was unusual for a ten-year-old to die like Suzanna did, and that they mustn't dwell on the subject of death so long; but she found she couldn't move. She lay motionless on the lounge, her face turned away from the sun, tears falling from her eyes.

They would surely change the mood of the conversation now, she thought, but Krista leaned against the fence and said, "I've never had a friend die before, have you, Missey?"

"Yeah . . . remember my friend Danny? He was at our sixth birthday party? Well, he had cancer and was sick a long time; but he's the only one I know who died. My mom said it was a blessing when he died because he was in pain all the time."

Nancy felt an aching hurt as she remembered Danny blowing out the birthday candles and entering into the games in spite of his pain. She thought with a gentle smile of Krista and Missey and how inseparable they had been since the Iversons had moved next to them five years before. They were like twins, sharing birthday parties, begging to "sleep over" or to "stay for dinner . . . just this once." They trailed each other everywhere and were even in the same classes at school.

Nancy treasured her friendship with Janie more than she could say, for they had been through a lot of joy and too much sorrow together. Janie's quiet, gentle care for her son caught at Nancy's heart. She wondered how she would react if one of her children had been born handicapped in some way, then quickly shut out the thought. If it hurt this badly to even think about, how must it feel to know your child would never develop properly or to see him waste away in pain as Danny had done?

Krista was talking, and though Nancy felt like an eavesdropper, she turned her head to hear the words. "Missey, why do you think God let Suzanna and Danny die? They were only little kids!"

"Mmmm . . . I dunno. But my mom says that God always has a reason for everything, and even if we don't understand, we have to trust that He knows best."

"I know but. . . ." Krista was frowning, "they were pretty young to die."

The hot sun was suddenly unbearable, and Nancy wanted to move, but she was transfixed. Missey was quoting her and she remembered so well the night after Danny's death when she had talked to Missey about God's perfect timing. Now Missey was repeating her words to Krista. "My mom says that God's timing is always perfect. In the Bible it says, 'a time for everything . . . a time to be born and a time to die.'"

"Does it really say that in the Bible? Where is it?"

Missey shook her head. "I can't remember. Eccl-e-act-is or

something like that. My mom showed it to me."

"But it's hard to understand just the same." Krista was still talking as Nancy drifted off to sleep, and when she awakened a short time later a cooling breeze had sliced through the hot air, softly rippling the water across the pool. It was too late for a dip; it was time to start dinner. She walked quickly into the house, but thoughts of death kept slipping in and out of her mind. When she was a child, she had never known anyone who had died; to hear her daughter discuss death so freely left her shaken.

That night when Missey was in bed, Nancy stood by her bed ready to snap off the light when suddenly she sat down and kissed her daughter's cheek. "I guess Krista must be feeling sad right now after having lost a good friend."

"Oh, no, mom, she's not." Missey turned over and not a trace of sadness shone in her dark eyes. "She called me tonight and said she thought about it after we talked, and even though she'll miss Suzanna, she knows that she is in heaven with Jesus and is really happy there."

There were no profound words to leave with Missey, Nancy thought as she shut the door behind her. Missey had said it all.

Perhaps neither of them would have remembered that conversation about death; it might never have had any significance at all if it had been just another summer, another August—but it wasn't. It was Krista's very last summer on earth, and she would have the desire of her ten-year-old heart—to die with her family and be buried next to them.

It was a perfect day. Blue skies stretched across the horizon without a cloud in sight, and the distant mountains were etched clearly against the heavens like a painted landscape. The air was warm but clear and sparkling after a summer shower had cleared away the smog.

Scattered tables decorated with brightly colored flowers were set up in the manicured backyard of the Grimes' home, and throughout the house there were signs of a festive occasion. It was Paul and June's fortieth wedding anniversary party, for which Gerry and Janie were hosts. Janie had planned the details with Carole the week before at the cabin, and now everything was falling into place perfectly.

Janie was lovely in the long beige dress Carole had loaned

Last family photograph taken at the anniversary party—Gerry, Janie, Paul and June Grimes, Krista, Jeffrey

her, smiling and hugging old friends of her parents, people she hadn't seen for years. Gerry was handsome in his blue suit, standing by her side as they greeted the guests.

Paul and June felt rich beyond words. Their friends filled their home, chatting with each other, reminiscing over old times with sudden outbursts of laughter at some nearly forgotten memory.

"Krista is so pretty, Janie. She is looking more like you every day."

"Jeff, my goodness, how you've grown! You look just like your father."

Nathan, as though an angel had touched him, slept through the afternoon, allowing Janie the freedom of chatting with old friends.

Gerry snapped pictures, running from the backyard to the living room, catching informal shots and more elegantly posed ones of Paul and June standing beside a three-tier cake as they had forty years before.

When the first sign of dusk appeared, the guests began to leave, kissing Paul and June and wishing them them many more years of joy. Several went to give Janie a special hug. "You're growing more beautiful each year, Janie, in every way." Janie smiled, the sparkle back in her lovely blue eyes.

When the door was closed on the last guests, Gerry and Paul cleared the outdoor tables while Janie and her mother stacked dishes to be placed in the dishwasher later, chatting together about the joyful afternoon of reunion.

Nathan awakened, and June ran to pick him up. He was calm, which was unusual after a nap, and Janie thought he seemed almost normal today as he lay his sleepy head on his grandmother's shoulder.

"Let's take the kids to MacDonald's for a hamburger," Paul suggested. "They're probably hungry." Jeff and Krista quickly agreed. They piled into Gerry's Renault and rode the short distance to MacDonalds. They found an outdoor table, and Paul took the children with him to order.

Gerry was unusually cheerful today, looking forward to Tuesday when they would head for Big Bear and a time of relaxation as a family.

Janie held Nathan, feeding him first, and thought about how proud she was of her children. Everyone had congratulated them on their beautiful manners.

It seemed such a happy, peaceful moment that words of gratitude and love were flowing in abundance.

"You know, mom," Janie said, "I think it would be fun to celebrate our twenty-fifth and your fiftieth wedding anniversary together making it a double celebration."

"No, mommy," Krista broke in emphatically, "you won't be able to do that."

"Well, Krista, why not?" Janie laughed.

"Because we'll all be gone then. Jesus will be back for us before that."

Janie smiled and hugged her daughter. "Maybe you're right, honey."

They were getting ready to get into the car when June stopped suddenly, turned and touched Janie's cheek. "Janie, you've been a wonderful daughter. I wish I'd had a dozen like you."

Janie hugged her mother in a warm embrace. "Oh, mom, you have lots of daughters. All of my girl friends love you as though they were your daughters."

"That's a sweet thing to say. Janie, it was a lovely party. How can we ever thank you and Gerry—and for the gift too! And the card was priceless. We'll cherish it always." June smiled, remembering the bright yellow card with dancing butterflies scattered over the words. She had opened Gerry and Janie's gift first and read the card to her guests. It was about love that holds a family together, love that makes a house into a home, love that makes memories to share. Below the words Janie had written, "We wish you God's best for however many more years He gives you together before He comes again."

Now they climbed into the white Renault, and when they arrived at the Grimes' home, they stood in the driveway reluctant to part. But it was time to say good-by.

Paul held Nathan, hugging him tightly, then gave him back to Janie and reached down to kiss Krista. He shook hands with Gerry and Jeff. "Can't wait to see those pictures. They'll be wonderful keepsakes."

"Good-by, mom and dad. We'll call before we leave on Tuesday and see you as soon as we get back," Janie called.

"Take care now and . . . Janie," June had her hand on the door and looked straight into her daughter's eyes, "promise me you'll rest this week at the cabin. Rest, honey. You've been working so hard."

"I promise, mom." Janie blew a kiss to her mother. "I promise I'll rest."

Paul and June waited until Gerry had turned the car around and headed toward home. They watched while he waited at the stop sign at the end of their street. Jeff and Krista were waving from the back seat, and June saw Janie's face for just a flash as she half-turned, waved, smiled, and blew another kiss. Just as the car turned the corner, she caught a glimpse of Nathan waving his chubby hand in a final good-by.

It had been a lovely day with family and friends, a day Paul and June Grimes would relive and treasure in their memories forever. Paul reached for June's hand and held it tightly. They stood in the night air for a time until a sudden breeze caused June to shiver.

Paul put his arm around her as they walked to the porch. "I was just remembering something Janie said to me yesterday. While you were at the hairdresser's, Janie and I were decorating the tables and she was talking about the grace of God. She said she was newly aware of His unconditional love; even when we deserve punishment, He keeps extending His grace; and because God forgives that way, we should forgive in the same way."

June stood on the porch looking up at the clear, star-filled night. She didn't say anything at that moment, but in the days ahead that conversation about the forgiving grace of God would come to their minds over and over.

There was no way for Paul and June to know as they walked contentedly into their home that it was one of the last moments of such serene happiness they would know for some time.

On Tuesday night, Paul and June were unusually tired from Sunday's anniversary party, and by 7:30 they were ready for bed.

Paul checked all the doors, opened their bedroom window, and by the time he slipped into bed, June was nearly asleep. He could hear the faint hum of the air conditioner next door when suddenly he was jolted by the sound of a distant voice calling softly, *"Daddy!"* He jerked himself to alertness, jumped from bed, and walked quickly to the window. "What time did you say the kids left, honey?" he called to June. She turned sleepily.

"They called to say good-by around four o'clock," she answered.

Paul turned from the window, a trickle of apprehension touching him. He was sure now. It was Janie's voice calling out to him as though she were there in the room. But if they had left at four and called to say good-by, how could it be? His imagination must be tricking him. He was wide awake now and fragments of memories from the party were floating through his mind. He smiled in the darkness, remembering.

Krista in her long pink dress, a lavender orchid pinned on her shoulder, had looked like Cinderella at the ball, he thought, so like Janie when she was her age.

And how beautiful Janie was, her old sparkling self, vivacious and effervescent, dazzling everyone with her unique charm.

Gerry had been right by her side helping her greet guests, listening adoringly while he heard over and over what a cute baby she had been and what a sweet and beautiful woman she had become.

June was as lovely as the day they were married. June and Janie were his two girls, and he loved them both dearly.

And Jeff—what a fine young man he was and how gentlemanly he had been at the party, greeting the guests with an unusual maturity for a boy not quite twelve.

Fortunately little Nathan had been able to sleep through the noise of the party, allowing Janie free time to enjoy old friends. It had been one of the loveliest days Paul could remember. He wanted to hold it fast in his memory forever.

Their little Janie had grown up to give them all they could ever desire. It seemed so long ago that he and June had prayed God would give them "one little baby," and how he remembered those long months of pain June endured to bring Janie into the world. But it had been worth it all. She had made their lives rich and happy beyond words.

She never complained about Nathan, even though Paul knew she was getting little sleep. One weekend they had kept Nathan when Janie had the flu, and he knew from experience the sleepless nights and restlessness that plagued the little boy. But Janie just went on helping out at the church and counseling young people or other mothers with Down's syndrome children. And what an added blessing it was that they lived close by. Gerry could have taken a church in the East someplace, but God had given them the joy of having their children and grandchildren near them.

Paul never told anyone, but he worried about Nathan's future. He knew Janie wasn't strong, and he noticed that her limp was coming back again. He wondered how she could care for Nathan when he grew tall and still had the mind of a child. He tried not to think beyond each day, but it was hard not to be concerned for Nathan and difficult not to wonder how far he really would develop. He was glad Gerry was strong and so in love with Janie; Paul was sure Gerry would always be at Janie's side, helping her, and that gave him a certain measure of peace.

He dozed fitfully, awaking abruptly at intervals, his mind alert as though something had roused him. Finally he was on the edge of sleep, although he never could be sure whether he was dreaming or awake when the telephone pierced the stillness of the night with a sharp ring. June stirred a little, and Paul reached for the phone beside their bed.

He glanced at the clock before he picked up the receiver. *Who on earth would be calling at midnight?* he wondered, and said a gruff hello into the mouthpiece.

"Mr. Paul Grimes?" The voice was unfamiliar and seemed to be coming from a distance.

"Yes, I'm Paul Grimes," he answered.

"This is the California Highway Patrol."

Paul's heart began to hammer, and he half-turned to look at June. She was sitting up now, looking at him inquiringly.

"Do you know a Helen Jane Iverson?"

"Yes, she's my daughter."

"Do you know a Gerald Iverson?"

"Yes, he's my son-in-law."

"Do you know a Krista Iverson?"

"Yes, she's my granddaughter."

"Do you know a Nathan Iverson?"

"Yes, he's my grandson."

Paul pressed the receiver to his ear, listening to the monotone on the other end of the line telling him something he refused to comprehend.

"I'm sorry to have to tell you, but all of them have been killed in an auto accident at the cutoff on the way out of Big Bear. Jeffrey Iverson is alive and in Loma Linda Hospital."

The word escaped his lips. *"Killed?"*

June cried out and began to scream, but over her loud wails he could still hear the officer informing him in a matter-of-fact voice of the details of the accident. There had been a head-on crash with a pickup truck; all of the bodies had been removed. Did he want to go to the morgue and identify their bodies?

Bodies? The bodies of his precious children and grandchildren taken to a cold morgue. Numbness was spreading to his chest, constricting his throat. He thanked the officer and hung up abruptly. June was standing beside him, but he kept hearing heart-rending screams, as though they were coming from a distance. His arms went around her, but he felt as though he were being ripped apart.

"Oh, no! My baby . . . my babies . . . Oh dear God, no!"

The doorbell rang sharply, and June turned toward the door in a daze. She stared hollowly at their neighbor who was clutching her robe about her and saying in a frightened voice, "What happened? We heard screams."

Paul told her the news in a voice that was scarcely a whisper.

"All gone?" She drew in a quick, unbelieving breath.

"Jeff is alive."

June sat heavily on the sofa, her eyes glazed and staring. She heard many voices and knew that as dawn was filtering through the windows, neighbors and friends were gathering in her living room.

Someone was offering her a glass of water, and she stared at it numbly. She shook her head and felt tears coming once more.

She heard Paul dialing a number and talking brokenly to a close friend. "He'll be here soon," he told June, but nothing, *nothing* could comfort her. All the words of comfort in the world could not bring her family back.

The early dawn became a nightmare of people standing over her. She saw drawn faces, tear-filled eyes, and then for moments nothing at all. Her own weeping began to crescendo into loud sobs, shaking her body with a terrible intensity.

What could possibly bring the slightest bit of consolation ever again? All they had been through the past two years since Nathan's birth seemed like nothing compared to this inconsolable anguish.

Paul glanced at his watch. Dawn was lighting up the summer sky just as if it were another ordinary day. He thought of Janie as a baby, so beloved; as a little girl, brown curls dancing; as a teen-ager, bringing joyful life into their home; and as a young wife and mother, growing more beautiful each day. He remembered how she used to call him at bedtime when she was a little girl, especially in the summer when it was still light.

"Daddy," she would call, "I want to get up. It's not night-time yet."

"Go to sleep, honey," he'd answer back. "It'll be dark in a little while."

Tears were gushing down his cheeks, and suddenly he remembered back just a few hours. A small voice calling *"Daddy"* as he was about to fall asleep. Was it his imagination or had Janie called his name just before the blinding crash? He put his head between his hands and sobbed without restraint, his shoulders shaking with grief.

He felt June touch him, and they clung together sobbing. It was hard to believe they could ever find solace again in this world.

The whirling helicopter made its ascent, but before it could reach the Loma Linda Hospital, Krista closed her eyes forever. The attendant's face was grave as he glanced at the boy, but Jeff remained conscious, dazed, unable to say a word. The helicopter landed in the heliport at the hospital, and Jeff was rushed into emergency.

In a dim haze he saw doctors bending over him, probing his body for injuries and asking him questions he could not answer. He heard someone say his shoulder was broken and that he would need surgery. He listened to another doctor say he was in shock and would not be able to be operated on for a time.

Jeff heard the starched rustle of a nurse enter his room and closed his eyes tightly. Finally he felt a sharp needle in his hip, pushing him over the brink into a deep sleep.

When Jeff awakened the next morning, his grandparents were standing over his bed, but Jeff didn't speak. He was afraid of questions he couldn't answer, couldn't even remember. His mind had shut off the moment of screams inside the car, the terrible sound of the collision, his lifeless parents and little brother Nathan. He tried not to think of Krista's moans beside him on the ride to the hospital. He pushed the fresh memory to the back of his subconscious to surface at another time.

"He must be told before surgery," the doctor informed Paul on the second day after the accident. "He's a troubled boy, and it would be better if he knew the truth." Paul nodded. He knew instinctively that he must be the one to tell Jeff.

June slipped her arm through Paul's on the ride in the elevator to the fourth floor, squeezing it as though to offer him the added strength he would need.

Jeff's face seemed as white as the pillows under him when his grandparents walked into the room. June leaned down and kissed him on the forehead, then took his hand and asked how he felt today. Was the pain very bad? Paul ran his hand slowly across the guardrail of the bed.

"Jeff," Paul kept his voice under control although his insides were trembling, "we have something to tell you." Jeff still didn't look at him, so Paul touched his hand gently. "Jeff, the Lord has taken your dad and mom and Krista and Nathan to be with Himself."

The moment he said the words, the truth of it struck Paul with appalling force. His grief was so intense that his voice broke, and he began to sob, bending down over Jeff as if he could protect him from the terrible hurt. Paul was unaware that tears were rolling down Jeff's cheeks, and that June was quietly wiping them away, while holding a tissue to her own eyes.

A hand touched Paul's wet cheek. It was Jeff reaching to him in comfort.

"Don't cry, grandpa. It's all right. I already knew. I just knew that even if my mother was hurt real bad she'd call me somehow. I just knew they were all gone."

The memory of another voice from another time slid into June's conscious thoughts. It was Janie's small, sweet voice comforting her on an ambulance ride many years ago: "It's okay, mommy, God must have a reason."

How many memories would come floating back that she could never shut off, memories flooding back to her in rapid succession? There was no place she could go that would not hold memories of Janie; she was in her heart. *Oh, God!* June cried out silently. *What possible reason could You have for taking my precious children and grandchildren?* Her world had been shattered, torn apart; and as she watched her husband weeping over Jeff, she knew his grief was as deep as hers. He had adored his only child ever since the moment thirty-five years ago when she had opened her blue eyes and looked at them. He had been a doting, loving father whose life revolved around his family.

Poor dear Jeff was lying there trying to comfort his grandfather. But who could ever heal *his* breaking heart? What could make up for the loss of his whole family, his home? June wondered if Jeff was thinking about the future—where he would live, who would care for him.

But Jeff's mind was on his immediate yesterdays—flashes of scenes of the last days with his family, preparing for their vacation. He remembered impatiently waiting for Krista to take her cat to Missey with instructions, his mother tenderly holding Nathan on her lap, and his father driving through the freeways telling him that they would be fishing the next day. His mind picked up fragmented scenes of that drive, of stopping at the cabin, of driving to the grocery store for film. He murmured a few words.

"What, Jeff?" Paul straightened, his face streaked with tears.

"If only dad had let me go back for gum," he repeated, and

suddenly the floodgate of tears opened and he began to cry aloud, "If he had only let me go back for gum, it wouldn't have happened . . . just one more minute and it wouldn't have happened."

Paul was silent, trying to control his trembling body. He knew he must bring words of comfort to Jeff right now, and as he spoke his own heart took refuge.

"They had an appointment, Jeff." Paul wiped his glasses thoughtfully. "Just like the Bible says, 'It is appointed unto man once to die.' So you see, God was right on time—not a minute too late nor a minute too soon."

Jeff didn't speak. He was remembering clearly the screams in the car, the lights racing toward them, the sudden crashing sound. His heart was too tender with fresh memories to answer his grandfather. He turned his head and let the tears roll down his cheeks, and when the nurse sedated him he gratefully fell into the arms of a deep, dreamless sleep.

Surgery was performed the next morning, and throughout the day both sets of grandparents sat by his bedside. Douglas and Kathryn Iverson had lost their only son whom they had adored, and it was impossible to think beyond their grief. It was important to stay close to Jeff, to see him, to touch him, for he was all that was left of their son—as impossible as that was to comprehend.

Saturday . . . the day of the funeral. Jeff lay still all day, his shoulder encased in a large cast, refusing to be comforted. Friends stayed with him, watching the sun rise, shine at its hottest, and disappear behind the mountains.

The outline of trees shaded his window, and that night if he turned his head just right, he could see the stars—thousands of them. He was glad he was alone in his room now for he wanted to look up at the summer sky and let his imagination soar to where his family had gone. God had taken them to their heavenly home. Now Jeff remembered that it had been nearly dark as they were driving down the mountain road. He wondered what heaven must be like. He knew there was no night there, but he wondered what they would do all the time. He tried to picture his mom and dad holding Nathan; and if he shut his eyes tight, he could see his mom's face all lit up with joy when she saw that Nathan was well. He imagined his dad throwing Nathan up in the air and saying, "He's healed! He's whole! Nathan is well!"

He smiled, thinking of Krista running around trying to find her friend Suzanna, and when she found her they would laugh and play together and run through green meadows; and . . . Jeff's smile broadened . . . how would Krista ever manage without her animals?

And Jeff thought about Jesus. He wondered if He came up to newcomers and put His arms around them. He bet He did for his folks so He could tell them about him and how lonely he was, and maybe his mom would say, "Well, why not send another angel to help Jeff right now?" And God would give the order and an angel would come floating down to help him.

His folks would be so happy to be together, and God had left him on earth because He knew he was strong enough to take it. He thought about that until dawn brought morning light and a flurry of activity, which meant nurses were on their way to take his temperature and pester him about a bath and brushing his teeth.

Jeff could hardly wait until visiting hours. He had something to tell his grandparents . . . something he had been thinking about all night. He told them the minute they came in the door.

"Just think . . . God knew that dad would be so unhappy if mom had been killed. And what if Nathan had been killed and not mom. How would she feel? And Krista never would have made it without mom. And mom couldn't stand it if she had been left behind. So you see, I'm the only one that could take it.

God knew I was the strongest, so he left me."

It was a moment of profound tenderness, for Jeff was really saying, "I accept this. I can go on. I'll be all right."

Perhaps that night a special angel did touch Jeff's courage, for it was the beginning of his soul's healing.

Telephones were ringing all over La Crescenta and the foothill area and throughout the San Fernando Valley. The shock of the tragedy that had taken nearly a whole family had rocked the southern California area.

In the Davis home, Ron had left for work earlier than usual and Nancy was sleeping in when the telephone rang sharply, interrupting her dreams. She reached for the receiver and whispered a sleepy hello.

"Nancy? This is Mildred McClure. I hope I didn't wake you."

Nancy recognized the voice of her neighbor and wondered vaguely why she would be calling her at seven o'clock in the morning.

"It's okay, Mildred."

"I'm sorry to have to be the bearer of bad news, Nancy, but the Iversons were in a terrible automobile accident last night, and there is only one survivor."

Nancy sat up quickly, unable to comprehend what she had just heard. Mildred must be mistaken—why just yesterday Krista had brought over her kitten with written instructions for Missey on how to take care of her. And they had all stood on the sidewalk *just yesterday* and watched the Iversons load their small car to the brim with luggage and food for their vacation at Big Bear.

"Mildred . . . it can't be!" She was having trouble catching her breath. She kept hearing the words *only one survivor;* and though she didn't want to know who survived, she knew she must ask.

"Who, Mildred? Who survived?" She held her breath. How would Nathan ever make it without his adoring mother? Or Krista or Gerry without Janie? Her mind was whirling, but Mildred spoke tearfully now. "Only Jeff lived. He's in the Loma Linda Hospital with a broken shoulder."

"Thank you for calling, Mildred. I want to be the one to tell Missey." They spoke a few fragmented sentences, and Nancy replaced the receiver. She walked unsteadily to the hall, glancing with thankfulness at her children's closed bedroom doors. Then she walked back to her room, closed the door, and began to weep, her head buried in the pillow.

Her own children were sleeping soundly and safely in their beds while Krista and Nathan were . . . she couldn't bring herself to say it. She knew her awful sobbing would awaken her children, but she couldn't stop. Her dear, dear friend Janie, the most precious girl she had ever known, the person who had brought so much joy to her own life for the past five years . . . gone! Four people she had lived beside and grown to know and love . . . *all killed.* O God, how was it possible?

"Mom? Mom?" Michelle and Mike were standing at her bedroom door and looking at her wonderingly. "What's the matter?" Nancy called them into her room, and while they sat on the edge of the bed, she told them the shocking news. Their faces registered immediate disbelief.

"Oh, mom, what shall we tell Missey?" Michelle's sweet sixteen-year-old concern was for her younger sister. Mike was speechless. How terrible for Jeff. How awful to lose his whole family. What would he do if he lost his own mom and dad? His throat constricted, and he fought against tears. Fourteen-year-old boys didn't cry. But suddenly there was no way to keep them back. Nancy held her children close, as though they had become doubly precious, while each shed tears of deep mourning.

The incredible shock had made Nancy's head reel. She dialed Ron's office number and felt strength from hearing his voice, from knowing he was there to help her when she felt as though she couldn't step out of her room. Ron was stunned and silent for a long while.

"Don't tell Missey until I get home," he said shortly. "She's going to the lake today, right? Let her go, and we'll tell her together tonight. Now promise me, honey."

"Yes, Ron, I promise. I'll try not to even let on that anything's wrong. I just don't know what to tell her."

Nancy helped Missey get ready for her day at the lake. If she was absent-minded, Missey didn't notice in her excitement over the day ahead with her friends.

It seemed the day would never end. The telephone rang persistently, and shocked conversation continued throughout the afternoon until Nancy asked Michelle to answer further calls and quietly retreated to her room.

She opened her Bible to the comfort of the Psalms and fell to her knees. "Father," she started to pray aloud; but she couldn't control her voice or her thoughts, so silent cries of grief tumbled

139

from her heart to her heavenly Father. Grief for Jeff, for the parents of Gerry and Janie, and finally tears of grief for her own loss. She remembered Janie's face popping over the fence calling her to have a cup of coffee; she recalled the laughing Janie she had known before the terrible grief of Nathan had enveloped her.

No one had really understood the extent of care Nathan needed, the sleepless nights that tormented Janie, the long drives to therapy with a crying baby. Janie had kept a smiling face for her friends, and suddenly Nancy wished for just one moment to tell Janie how much she loved her, how she admired her, what an impact her life had been on her family. "Oh, Janie, I'll never forget you . . . never!" She asked God to give Ron and herself just the right words for Missey that night. She remembered Janie telling her about a verse she loved . . . about the death of God's children being precious in His sight.

Then the sudden realization came over Nancy that Janie's prayer for Nathan's healing had been answered. Now all of his tomorrows were taken care of.

That night Ron and Nancy gathered the family together in the den. "We have some sad news for you, Missey." Ron leaned over and took his daughter's hand. She sensed his serious look and her mother's tear-stained face and straightened up immediately.

"What is it?"

"It's about Krista, honey. She was in an accident." Ron cleared his throat, and Nancy concluded, "Missey, remember when you and Krista were talking about going to heaven someday and what it would be like?"

Missey nodded.

"Well, honey, it happened a little sooner than Krista imagined. Krista is with Jesus now. And Krista's mom and dad and Nathan."

Missey sat stone still, a look of unbelieving shock on her face.

"They were in an auto accident, honey," Ron explained.

"What . . . but why would God do that?"

"Missey, God has a plan for all of our lives, and His plan was to take Krista and her family to be with Him now."

Missey began to cry. "It's all my fault! Oh, mommy, if only I had talked to Krista one more minute when she brought the cat's food, they wouldn't have been in the accident."

Nancy held her daughter gently and explained once more that God's timing was perfect and that He had chosen that moment for them to go to be with Him.

"Look, honey, let's read this verse again together. Remember I read it to you before—in Ecclesiastes?" Nancy began to read aloud: "There is a right time for everything: a time to be born, a time to die."[1]

Missey nodded. "But what about Jeff? Who's going to take care of him? Is he hurt bad? How is he taking it? Oh, mommy, can Jeff live with us? Could we be his family?"

"God must have a special reason to leave Jeff here, honey. He knows Jeff is strong. And as for a home, Missey, there are many people who want Jeff. It will be his choice where he wants to live."

"Mommy," Missey's face was stricken, "I just thought of the Iversons and Grimes. How terrible for them. We've got to pray for them."

And they did. Holding hands, they spoke to God quietly about the empty place that would be left in all the bereaved hearts.

"Please fill the emptiness with Yourself, Lord," Nancy concluded the prayer.

"I keep thinking about what Krista told me about her friend Suzanna—that she would miss her so much but that she knew she was in heaven with Jesus and so happy. I know now that

---

[1]Ecclesiastes 3:1-2 LB

God gave Krista those words to tell me so I would remember them now and not feel so bad."

God had prepared Missey that day the two girls had had a conversation about death. Every word was remembered and intact in Missey's mind.

Nancy thought of something Janie had told her one day not long ago. "Nancy," she said, "the whole purpose, the whole meaning of our lives as Christians is to bring glory to God; so whether I live or die, that is my desire."

There was little doubt that Janie's life had brought many people to Jesus Christ. But how, Nancy wondered, could her death be glorifying to Him?

She might never know the full purposes of God, but she was sure that someday, somehow it would be true. God would be magnified through the death of Gerry, Janie, Krista, and Nathan; and Gerry and Janie's life verse would go on and on, as God received glory and honor for His mercy and truth's sake.

That very day the telephone rang in another home, and Pam Nelson was unprepared for the words that would sting forever in her memory. "Pam"—it was her mother calling—"oh, how I dislike telling you this, honey, but your friend Janie was in an accident. Her whole family was killed except their son Jeff."

Pam felt her knees buckle, and her head began to reel. "Janie? Dead . . . and?" She listened to the horrifying details in numb silence. When she replaced the receiver, she was weeping aloud. "O merciful God, what . . .?" She held Shelley more gently than ever, rocking her while she softly wept tears of grief.

If all the things Janie had said about God were true, then the tears were not for them but for herself. They were with their heavenly Father now, and Janie's dream had come true. Nathan was well. And now Janie could rest forever. She remembered Janie's last words once more, "I'm ready now for whatever God has for us in the future." *Oh, Janie,* Pam thought, *now you have what God had for you . . . perfect rest. Rest, Janie, rest in peace.*

Gerry's prayer the week of Shelley's birth came flooding through her mind. "Father," he had prayed, "please let Pam have Your peace through this suffering, and give us all peace."

They had peace now. Pam was weeping and letting the tears fall down her cheeks without wiping them away. She would never forget Janie Iverson nor the sweetness she had brought into her life when she needed help in the most desperate way.

At the memorial service Pam whispered brokenly to Paul and June, "Gerry and Janie touched our lives for such a short time, but they made the biggest impression of any couple we have ever known. Janie and I looked into the future and wondered about our children. Janie told me she didn't care if Nathan ever did anything spectacular. She just wanted him to be able to care for himself someday. Now she doesn't have to worry about his future."

That night Pam opened her desk drawer and took out the poem Janie had handed her the day they had coffee together. She read the words through eyes blinded by tears:

HEAVEN'S SPECIAL CHILD

A meeting was held quite far from earth.
"It's time again for another birth,"
Said the angels to the Lord above.
"This special child will need much love.

"His progress may seem very slow;
Accomplishment he may not show;
And he'll require extra care
From the folks he meets down there.

"He may not run or laugh or play;
His thoughts may seem quite far away.
In many ways he won't adapt,
And he'll be known as handicapped.

"Oh, let's be careful where he's sent,
We want this life to be content.
Please, Lord, find the parents who
Will do a special job for You.

"They will not realize right away
The leading role they are asked to play.
But with this child sent from above
Comes stronger faith and richer love.

"And soon they'll know the privilege given
In caring for this gift from heaven.
Their precious charge so meek and mild
Is heaven's very special child."

Anonymous

Pam smoothed the paper carefully, put it in a silver frame, and hung it over Shelley's bed, where she could see it each time she went into her baby's room. It would be a reminder of the brief encounter she had had with Janie Iverson and the love of God Janie had brought into her life.

On August 14, 1976, the memorial service for Gerry, Janie, Krista, and Nathan Iverson was held at the First Baptist Church in La Crescenta, the church where Gerry found Christ, was baptized as a teenager, grew in his faith, and returned to minister. There was standing room only.

Pastor Travaille was broken. Gerry had been like a son to him, and as he recalled cherished memories, there was a hush in the sanctuary. Each person's private thoughts were reflections of their own recollections of Gerry and Janie.

"One of the most delightful experiences around this church," Pastor Travaille began, "for the past few years on Sunday mornings was the experience of standing in the parking lot and seeing the Iverson family come to Sunday school—

Gerry and Janie Iverson unloading their car of all the Sunday school material, and Jeff and Krista and little Nathan running behind their parents.

"One Sunday not too long ago, a family I had never seen before saw the Iversons and exclaimed, 'What a darling family!' And I said, 'Not only a darling family, but a model family. Theirs is a home where in the very highest sense love really lives.'

"Some time ago I asked one of our college young people if it wouldn't be appropriate to have a class on marriage and the family. He thought for a moment and said, 'But, Pastor Travaille, we already have that.' I said, 'You do? Who is teaching you?' He replied, 'Pastor Iverson.' I said I didn't know Gerry was conducting classes on the family. He replied, 'Oh, he's not conducting classes or teaching us in words, but whenever we have a college affair the family always goes along. We have seen his devotion to his wife and hers to him, and we've learned more about Christian marriage and love and family from the Iverson family than could ever be taught in words.'

"Well . . . that's what the Bible says should be true of our leaders. They are to be examples to the flock. The Iversons were always together. I can't recall that I ever saw only one person in the little car. It always had the entire family in it, and I think it is significant that on their last trip they should all go together . . . with only Jeff left behind.

"Their ministry in the body of Christ has been of inestimable value. Janie was so supportive of Gerry, a true helpmate, ministering in the Sunday school department lovingly and efficiently.

"One of the teachers stopped by yesterday and said, 'Pastor Travaille, I think I should share something with you. Just a few weeks ago our lesson Sunday morning was about God's care for us, and Janie said, "Vacation time is coming, and who knows what may happen to us as we travel along the road. We should be aware that God watches over us even as He does the tiniest sparrow, and should something happen to any of us remember—*God always has a reason.*" '

"I count it as a great personal delight that Gerry came to a personal faith in Jesus Christ in this church, was baptized here, and came back to minister on the staff.

"I visited with Jeff yesterday, and he suggested that the song 'Now I Belong to Jesus' be sung. I was amazed that he should want that song because we don't sing it much around here any more; but Jeff told me that it was Gerry's favorite. And then I remembered—when Gerry was in high school and attending our Bible study class at noon, he would always sing as loud as he could the words to that song. . . .

"Why, then, should his ministry be cut short? John the Baptist's ministry was cut short. He was only a young man when his life ended. And what did his disciples do? They went and told Jesus. And that is what we did when we heard about the Iversons: we got together last night and told Jesus and He comforted our hearts.

"There was a note on my desk this morning from one of our college students. He said, 'I asked Gerry about six months ago if Christians were protected from accidents. He replied, "Well, first of all a Christian is absolutely invincible as long as God wants him here on earth. But Christians are not immune from tragedy. Take, for example, Paul Little, the well-known author and speaker. He was killed in an auto accident last year, seemingly right in the midst of a successful career. For some reason the Lord said, 'Paul, this is as far as you have to run the race. You can come home now.'" Gerry used the example of Paul Little's death on several other occasions after that, and he always stressed that it was like the end of the race, which was expected to be a grueling marathon but turned out to be *only a mile*. An unexpected but pleasant way to end a race.'

"We say farewell now to our loving and dear friends, but we know that we have a living hope for we 'sorrow not, even as others which have no hope.'[1] Other religions offer the promise of survival of personality and some kind of hope of the preservation of the soul, but the Christian gospel alone promises resurrection—that all things will be new.

"Gerry and Janie Iverson were probably the most gracious human beings you could ever find, loving and tender and gentle and of great character . . . wonderful servants of Christ. But it is not on this that we base our hope of eternal life, for the Bible says, 'For by grace are ye saved through faith; and that not of yourselves: it is the gift of God: not of works, lest any man should boast.'[2] Not too long ago Gerry quoted to me that passage from Titus 3:5: 'Not by works of righteousness which we have done, but according to his mercy he saved us. . . .' It is by that grace and mercy of our blessed Savior that we say farewell with a blessed hope of meeting them again in the morning.

"Janie had inscribed in Gerry's wedding ring these beautiful words: 'Not unto us, O Lord, not unto us, but unto thy name give glory.'[3] That was their life verse. And we know as we labored with them that God indeed did glorify Himself through their lives; and we are confident He will do so now through their death."

The closing prayer, spoken directly to God the Father, brought a stillness throughout the gathered bereaving loved ones of Gerry and Janie and with the stillness came a sweet, sweet spirit of hope.

Our gracious God and our loving Father, we thank You that we do not stand alone here today, but that Your love has gathered us to Yourself to

---

[1] Thessalonians 4:13 KJV
[2] Ephesians 2:8, 9 KJV
[3] Psalms 115:1 KJV

offer us comfort; that You have promised peace, not as the world gives but only as You give; that although the earth be shaken and mountains cast into the sea, though day turn into night and night into day, You are there. Your love is constant, and Your love abides forever. We thank You that You have not left us comfortless or without understanding or insight into Your ways; and although we may not understand all that has transpired in these past days, we thank You and praise You that You do all things well, and not one thing has happened that your sovereign hand has not allowed. Father, You promised in Your Word that You would be a father to the fatherless and a mother to the motherless. We know You will be all of this for Jeff as he grows into young manhood.

Father, we pray for the man who drove the truck and for his nephew that their needs will be met. We do not know their relationship with You, Lord; but we pray that through these events they might come to trust You as their Savior and Lord and thereby find understanding and the true meaning of life. Lord, if there is a need for them to find forgiveness, grant it to them. Grant us all the ability to forgive.

We thank You for Your heavenly Son, who came to this earth to die for our sins, for we know that You, God, sense sorrow even more deeply than we do because You gave Your Son on our behalf. May we look at that example of love, draw strength to understand the sorrow to which You went, and then praise You and thank You for that love which is far beyond our own.

Gerry, Janie, Krista, and Nathan were laid to rest in Rose Hills Cemetery in Whittier, California.

In her deep grief at the memorial service, June turned to a friend and said brokenly, "Just think, one minute Janie was sitting with a mentally retarded baby on her lap wondering about his future, and the next minute she was in heaven with a completely whole child."

Vielka Kelly, the little girl who lived next to the Grimes during Janie's teen-age years, remembered those days in a glowing tribute to Janie addressed to Paul and June.

When my mother phoned me on Thursday morning to tell me that Janie, her husband, and two of their children had died in a car accident the previous Tuesday, a special part of me also died.

People I knew well had died before, but no one whom I loved as much and as deeply as Janie. I cried day and night for two weeks after that telephone call, partly out of selfishness, knowing Janie would no longer be available to talk with and to love and to be loved by.

Janie was beautiful inside and out. Her inner love for others caused everyone who knew her to adore her. Jane was my next-door neighbor for about ten years. I looked up to her as an older sister, and to me the name Janie meant love. . . . I was always a sick child and suffered with eczema, an ugly-to-look-at skin allergy. It covered me from head to toe, and I was always miserable, not only physically, but mentally because of the teasing and unkind remarks made by other children who refused to play with me and just kept away from me for fear that whatever I had must be catching. Even adults reacted this way toward me. Except for my family and maybe a few others, everyone kept his distance from me—except, of course, for Janie.

I don't remember the exact day I first met Janie. We moved next door to the Grimes family when I was about four years old. Janie baby-sat for my older brother, Stephen, and me almost every day. I remember the special things she did for me and the kindness, tenderness, and love she showed me. My happiest childhood memories were made possible by Janie.

Janie taught me how to ride a two-wheel bike. I was always afraid, but one day she took off the training wheel and said, "Okay, I'll be right beside you," and she ran with me, and soon I was riding by myself. . . .

Janie would always do special things for me. For example, when making chocolate-chip cookies, she would make special ones for me without the chocolate chips because I was allergic to chocolate.

I remember another day my mom asked Janie if she'd cut my hair—it was better for me to wear it short because of my skin allergies, and I hated it that way. Janie patiently cut my hair, and when she finished, I looked in the mirror and cried. Janie looked at me and said, "Gee, I thought I did a really good job. It looks nice." She just had a way about her that made everything seem all right.

On another occasion Janie's cat, Kelly, was ready to give birth to kittens, and Janie decided to help her. Instead of being happy, that ungrateful cat clawed Janie so bad she had to go to bed and a doctor was summoned. I went over to visit her and sat on her bed, when in came the cat, who jumped on the bed, purring sort of apologetically. I remember making some sort of derogatory remark about the cat, to which Janie lovingly replied, "Oh, she's sorry now. It's okay, Kelly," and she petted her with the same love as before. . . .

I have so many wonderful memories of Janie and many incidents come to my mind like hearing her laugh and play with my brother and me or her taking the time to make me a special pompon when she was busy practicing for her cheerleading.

All too soon, Janie was getting married to a young seminary student named Gerry Iverson. I remember watching her come down the aisle after just being married. She was smiling and tears of happiness rolled down her cheeks.

I didn't hear from Janie very often after her wedding—usually just the once-a-year Christmas card. However, I remember seeing her, Gerry, and their infant son, Jeff, one day while she was visiting her parents. . . .

Janie and Gerry came to my wedding in June 1972. I remember standing outside the church after just being married and people gathering around congratulating us when suddenly there was Mrs. Grimes. She said, "Look who's here." Then Janie appeared. I remember screaming, "Janie!" What a joy to see her again and have her come to my wedding.

I spoke with Janie on the telephone in July of 1976. I called her to say I was going to the fortieth wedding anniversary party she and Gerry were giving her parents.

Ironically, Janie said her mom wanted to celebrate her fortieth wedding anniversary because Mrs. Grimes didn't think she'd be alive in ten years for her fiftieth wedding anniversary. I asked her why her mom thought that, and she said she didn't know. Her mom was in good health and was a fairly optimistic person, except on this one point. She wanted a big party now instead of later.

Janie then went on to say how originally it was going to be a small party, but it had grown so much that she had sent out over two hundred invitations. Janie also said, "You know, my dad's so funny. He asked me if I thought anyone would come to the party. I said, 'Of course they'll come.'"

We also spoke of how fast time goes, and Janie said she'd been married for fifteen years—I couldn't believe it and Janie couldn't believe I had two children already.

My older child and Janie's youngest baby were almost the same age. I never spoke to Janie about her little Nathan because he was born with Down's syndrome. I was sad that Janie had an abnormal child, although I knew that no one would be a more loving and understanding mother than Janie.

The last time I saw Janie was at her parents' home for the celebration of their fortieth wedding anniversary. It was sort of nostalgic for my parents and me to go back to the "old neighborhood." I couldn't wait to see Janie—I found her, and for a moment she stood staring, then said, "Vielkita!" (her favorite name for me). "I feel so old when I see you kids," she said. "You're so grown up!" I hugged her and told her she hadn't changed a bit; she looked exactly the same as I remembered her as a child.

We met Janie's lovely daughter Krista, who looked to me just like a younger version of Janie, and her son Jeff, now a tall young man. I asked if we could see Nathan. My mom, dad, and I followed Janie to see him. We went in the room, and there was baby Nathan fast asleep in a playpen. He was beautiful, and I commented about his having blond hair. Janie said, "We're very thankful to have such a healthy boy."

Janie was always thankful to God for everything she had. Her mom told me that Janie had gone into shock when Nathan was born and was found to be abnormal, but later she told her mom, "You know, God sent me that child for a purpose."

In my mind the purpose might have been to have Janie encourage and work with other mothers who had children like Nathan. Janie was in my opinion a saint, and her love for God easily spread to others, helping them with life here on earth. . . .

Later on, as we were leaving and saying our good-bys, I asked Janie to come visit and she said, "Yes, I really will come by the next time I take Nathan to school. It's not too much further to your home." I left, beaming with the happy anticipation of her visiting me and meeting my children.

If only we could look into the future, but of course we cannot.

The memorial service given Janie and her family was the most beautiful one I have ever attended. The large church was full of people and, arriving just in time for the beginning of the service, my husband and I found there was standing room only.

As I stood there listening to the eulogies, it was impossible to hold back the tears. A table had been set up in the front of the church with a recent photograph of the Iverson family; and four roses, each a different color with a matching ribbon, sat along both sides of the family portrait.

Janie probably would not like people making a fuss over her after her death, but if you knew Janie, you'd want to let the world know of the happiness and richness she gave to others.

I am thankful for having been blessed with knowing Janie and loving her and having her help me through those difficult childhood days. Janie helped me to live a happier life. She made me feel loved and needed, and I loved her deeply for that reason.

I think of Janie almost every day now and miss her. Janie will always be with me—in my mind and in my heart.

The words Janie had spoken to her father of God's unconditional love and forgiving grace helped bring deliverance from bitterness to the bereaved family. They not only freely forgave the man who had driven the truck, but Carole MacLane corresponded with him, offering words of comfort to his sorrowing, troubled mind.

One time Janie had found a verse in Psalm 116 and exclaimed to a friend, "Listen to this: 'Precious in the sight of the LORD is the death of his saints.' How unbelievably beautiful to know that when a Christian dies it is *precious* to the Lord!" Janie was overwhelmed at the beauty of the very thought that a death could be precious to God.

Now that verse was fulfilled. How precious in God's sight was that moment after the deafening crash of steel upon steel, that moment at dusk when God called His precious children home . . . home before dark.

Epilogue

Jeffrey Iverson was released from the Loma Linda Hospital in September and began junior high school that fall. He chose to make his home with his parents' dear friends Don and Carole MacLane. Jeff lives in his old neighborhood, attends the church where his father ministered, and has his same friends.

The MacLanes have three other children: Lori, eighteen, Kurt, fifteen, and Mike, twelve. Jeff and Mike are "Best buddies." Don MacLane is a fire captain who has plenty of time to spend with his boys, taking them to their cabin in Big Bear to hunt and fish or participating with them in all kinds of sports. Don MacLane has become "dad" to Jeff, and Carole is "mom."

Jeff received over three hundred cards and letters after the accident, reminding him how dearly loved his parents were; and he himself will never forget his family and the wonderful love they gave him. Jeff talks lovingly about Nathan, for he remembers the heartache and joy that little boy brought into their home. He says he is glad Krista is with his mother and dad. He speaks of his father with great pride, and a tenderness sweeps over his face when he remembers his mother.

Recently he was able to write the following testimony of forgiveness in a school essay:

> There was a man sitting at home with his twelve-year-old nephew. The man had a few beers, but wasn't planning on driving. He got a phone call that his office was on fire. He got in the truck with his nephew and they rushed to the office. On the way they had a head-on collision with a car. In this car were a minister, his wife, their son, their daughter, and younger son. The minister, his wife, daughter, and younger son were killed. Only the eleven-year-old boy survived. (The man and his nephew weren't seriously hurt.) The nephew and the minister's son shared a room in the hospital for a couple of days. They became friends. The man was tested at the site of the accident and was found to be legally drunk. The man was charged with manslaughter and felt very guilty.
>
> If you read a story like this in the newspaper, the man would look like an awful person. But this man was really good at heart. So I say people are both good and bad at heart. (By the way, I was the eleven-year-old boy.)

One night just before Christmas Jeff was standing on the porch and looking up at the clear, cold sky when Carole joined him.

There was a long silence, but when Jeff spoke, Carole was assured that he had met his tragedy with a growing acceptance and quiet strength. He said wistfully, "Just look how bright the stars are. My dad sure must be having a hard time adjusting his light meter."

Da'